This journal holds pieces of a heart in healing.

If found please contact:

Because some journeys are too sacred to lose.

A tool

Your ***closure***

When you choose peace, it comes with a lot of goodbyes, and this is one of them.

—RISING JOURNEY

Start your Rising *Journey*

The Rising Journey Sanctuary

The Noclosure Journal gives you structure. The Rising Journey Community gives you support.

You don't have to walk this path alone. The Sanctuary is a private circle, a space to breathe, to be witnessed, to speak when it feels like too much, and to be held by women who understand. It's where stories unfold in real time, heartbreak is met with softness, and sisterhood becomes part of your healing rhythm.

Whether you're on Day One or Day Twenty-One, there will be moments when emotions rise, questions surface, or silence feels too heavy to hold by yourself. This is where you can lean in. Rising is deeply personal, but it was never meant to be solitary. This is your space to *Process, Build,* and *Rise* together. A place to be seen, heard, supported, and reminded that you are not alone. Return when the echoes of the past rise. Come back when your heart asks for structure. Contribute when your voice is ready.

Share. Ask. Cry. Celebrate. Heal. This is healing while you heal.

Scan the QR code to join instantly

RISING JOURNEY COMMUNITY

Healing is lighter when you don't walk it alone.

Rising Journey

LEGAL DISCLAIMER

This journal is designed for personal growth, reflection, and emotional wellness. It draws from lived experience and commonly recognized healing practices, but it is not affiliated with or endorsed by any clinical or medical authority. The content is not intended to replace professional psychological or medical advice. If you're experiencing emotional distress or a mental health crisis, please consult a licensed therapist or medical professional. If you are in danger or in need of urgent support, contact emergency services or a crisis line in your area.

All reflections, tools, and language in this journal are original and rooted in personal healing. Any resemblance to existing work is unintentional and reflects shared themes within the wellness space. No part of this publication may be copied, distributed, or reproduced by any means without written permission from the author, except for brief quotes used for non-commercial purposes or reviews, with proper credit.

FIRST EDITION
ISBN: 978-1-0695792-0-1
Published independently by Rising Journey

JOIN THE JOURNEY:
@risingjourney.co | Rising Journey Community

Dedication

For every woman who was lied to, gaslit, cheated on, abandoned, or broken by someone who claimed to love her. For the one who gave everything and was left emptied, unseen, or with nothing. For the one left in silence, carrying questions no one ever stayed long enough to answer. What was withheld does not define you. It opens the way for what was always meant for you. You are worthy of healing, of a reset rooted in truth, of a beginning marked by clarity, grace, and peace. This journal holds what they never said, and guides you to rise into all you have always deserved.

This isn't just a story of heartbreak.
This is Noclosure, a sacred, intentional Rising Journey.
A space to heal without the apology.
To move forward without the explanation.
To honor what was never acknowledged,
and reclaim the parts of you that were never fully seen.
You don't need closure to begin again.
You already know the truth.
And that's enough to start healing.

Hey beautiful soul,

I wish I could give you a hug. I know how hard it's been.

I created this journal because I lived the pain of a relationship that ended without clarity. I know the search for answers in silence. The ache for closure that never comes. The replaying of conversations. The quiet habit of questioning yourself, justifying their behavior, and carrying emotions no one stayed long enough to help you name.

This journal is the tool and structure I wish I had then. Not empty positivity, but a sincere, science-informed Method. Built from lived experience. Rooted in trauma research. Shaped by the kind of wisdom you only gain by surviving it. What I learned through that experience is simple: healing requires structure. Time alone does not create wisdom. Meaning does.

Some stories end without reasons. Without goodbyes. When they do, a choice appears. To keep searching outward for meaning, or to turn inward and create it for yourself. This journal exists to support that inward turn. To slow the experience down long enough for insight to form. To process before beginning again. Healing here is treated as a deliberate practice, one that honors the experience, gathers its lesson, and allows you to move forward with clarity rather than repetition.

You deserve the right tools. You deserve time devoted to your healing. You deserve understanding that brings steadiness. You deserve to break patterns and build from clarity and strength. You deserve a future shaped by self-trust and the standards you choose to live by.

Thank you for trusting this process.
Thank you for deciding your healing matters.
You deserve the love you give so freely.

Hassania

Contents

Visual Compass

ICONS THAT GUIDE YOUR NOCLOSURE JOURNEY

The 21·7·7·7 Journey

Four phases of the Noclosure Method.

ICON	PHASE	MEANING
	PHASE 1	Process: Letting go of what no longer serves.
	PHASE 2	Build: A homecoming to self—restoring truth and energy.
	PHASE 3	Rise: Ascending with clarity, grounded in earned wisdom.
	BECOMING	Identity work and standards that shape what comes next.

Daily Rhythm

Release. Reframe. Rewire.

ICON	PRACTICE	MEANING
	The 21·7·7·7 Method	A 21-minute practice to Release · Reframe · Rewire
	RELEASE	Letting go, through reflection, writing, and Release.
	REFRAME	Seeing a new, shifting perspective, rewriting the story.
	REWIRE	Embedding truth, creating new, life-giving patterns.

Navigation

Markers that guide your movement.

ICON	MARKER	MEANING
	RADIANT SUN	Marks a key rising moment or point of integration.
	WISDOM MARKER	Highlights grounding truths to carry forward.
	ARROW SET	Guides your flow to the next page.
	SINGLE ARROW	Bridges to an introductory or framing page.
	BREATH CUE	Invites a pause, a breath, for nervous system calm.

Tool Icons

Core healing tools and resets.

ICON	TOOLS	MEANING
	TRACE SYSTEM	Tracks micro-habits that strengthen boundaries, self-trust, and regulation.
	IDENTITY ANCHOR	21 principles to live by, anchored in lived wisdom, boundaries, and becoming.
	NIGHT SAFETY	Three-step ritual to release mental weight, find clarity, and reach resolution when sleep won't come.
	ILLUSION BREAKER	Sets fantasy and truth side by side, dissolving the illusion between them.
	THE SPIRAL RESET	A 6-step, real-time nervous system reset for emotional spirals. Steps: 1.Breathe · 2.Name · 3.Stop · 4.Forgive · 5.Live · 6.Anchor

Every tool is an anchor. Every page is a doorway. Healing is presence, consistency, and practice. A gentle remembering of who you are, and what you deserve, again and again. With each practice, with each ritual, you reclaim your choice, your rhythm, your rise.

—RISING JOURNEY

Before You Begin

Noclosure Journal was designed to meet you in real time, with structure, truth, and emotional safety. It's not a positive affirmations journal or a quick-fix notebook. It's a 21-day guided system rooted in *the 21·7·7·7 Method*: 21 days · 21 minutes · 3 steps · 7 minutes each.

It's a 21-day healing experience rooted in *the 21·7·7·7 Method.* Because emotional wellness is not optional, it's essential. Just as you nourish your body with intention, your nervous system deserves the same level of attention, and sophistication.

Every ending deserves a moment of stillness. The reflection. The healing. The return to you. The lessons gained, the experiences that taught.

How to Navigate Your Rising Journey

If you'd like to begin quickly, this page offers the essentials. If you want the deeper science and structure, you'll find it in the next section. But before you turn the page, know this:

These opening pages are the foundation you may have never received—the clarity, context, and nervous system grounding most healing spaces overlook.

They reveal why you feel stuck, how this *Method* supports your whole system, and what begins to shift when you stop chasing closure and start choosing peace. They also offer tools to build clarity, regulate your nervous system, and create a sense of safety.

Your healing is yours. If you'd rather skip ahead and return later, that's okay too.

Every day of this journal offers a structure rooted in *the 21·7·7·7 Method*—a daily rhythm designed to gently guide your nervous system through healing. You'll move through *Release* · *Reframe* · *Rewire* in a science-aligned sequence, designed to meet your nervous system exactly where it is.

Your 21-Minute Daily Rhythm

21·7·7·7

RELEASE · REFRAME · REWIRE

21 DAYS · 7 MINUTES · 7 MINUTES · 7 MINUTES

Every day you'll follow this simple structure: 7 minutes to *Release*, 7 minutes to *Reframe*, 7 minutes to *Rewire*. This daily rhythm is what keeps your healing steady and structured.

21 DAYS · 21 MINUTES · 3 STEPS · 7 MINUTES EACH

The Daily Practice: 21·7·7·7

(21 minutes total)

Release *7 min*	Write honestly about what you feel.
Reframe *7 min*	Notice the old story, then shift to a clearer truth.
Rewire *7 min*	Anchor with the new wisdom.

21 days. 21 minutes. 3 steps. The Noclosure Method mirrors the brain's own pathway for closure—from releasing to reframing to rewiring.

The 21–Day Journey

This journal is more than blank pages. It is a path. One that meets you where you are, and walks with you as you move forward. *The Noclosure Method* is not reflection alone, but a neuroscience–aligned framework for emotional repair, grounded in rhythm, repetition, and safety.

It mirrors the nervous system itself, moving through processing, integration, and renewal. Across 21 days, your journey unfolds through three phases of becoming: *Process* · *Build* · *Rise.* Each phase is designed to meet you where you are and carry you forward with clarity and intention.

The Three Phases of Healing

- Phase 1: *Process* (Days 1–7)
- Phase 2: *Build* (Days 8–14)
- Phase 3: *Rise* (Days 15–21)

This is the architecture of *Noclosure:* a daily method, built inside a 21–day journey. Phase by phase, this is how you rise.

The Tools Along the Way

Each phase, *Process* · *Build* · *Rise,* begins with the Trace System: a set of gentle, embodied micro–habits designed to rebuild core emotional patterns like boundaries, self–trust, and regulation.

Along the way, you'll also work with targeted tools—Night Safety, Spiral Reset, Illusion Breaker, and others—designed to meet you in your most vulnerable moments and return you to stability.

21 Days as a Shift

This is the Becoming Work, the structured, intentional plan that follows healing.

→ Compound Becoming System

→ 21 Lines I Will Live By

→ Final Reflections

The 21 days are not the end. They mark the beginning of understanding and Becoming. Closure shifts from something you seek to something you recognize and live by. This is where healing integrates into clarity, and what you've learned begins shaping who you are becoming.

Healing Is Not Linear

When emotions return, let the rituals anchor you. Healing is not linear. If you miss a day, simply begin again. To reconnect with your why, turn back to your Reality Check or Illusion Breaker and Commitment Contract.

This journal is designed to be returned to, not only in moments of pain, but at turning points of growth, from overwhelm to inner knowing guided by steady rhythm, quiet commitment, and a self–led clarity that no one can take away. Because closure isn't given, it's built, sustained, and *lived.*

Every ending calls for intention.
Every intention begins with a decision.
And every decision opens into a beginning.
This one is yours. Step into the work, into the rhythm, into the rise.
Welcome to Noclosure.

Welcome to Noclosure

You're holding this journal because something ended without really ending. The words you needed were never spoken. The clarity you deserved was replaced with silence, confusion, or half-truths that left you carrying the weight that was never yours to hold.

Maybe you were ghosted after months of connection. Maybe they slowly withdrew, leaving you to decode mixed signals and wonder what you did wrong. Maybe they stayed physically but disappeared emotionally, creating a hollow space where love used to live. Or perhaps there was betrayal, gaslighting, or promises that crumbled the moment you needed them most.

Whatever brought you here, one truth remains: you were left holding questions no one stayed long enough to answer. This journal isn't about getting those answers. It's about no longer needing them. You've probably replayed every conversation, analyzed every text, and searched for signs you missed. You've told the story to friends, therapists, and anyone who would listen, hoping someone could help it make sense.

You've waited for an apology that never came, an explanation, or a moment of accountability from someone who chose to walk away rather than face themselves. But here's what you're beginning to understand: their actions said more than any explanation ever could. And their silence, not their apologies—became your closure.

This isn't about blame or resentment. It's about reclaiming your heart and peace from those who were never capable of protecting it. Some people may love you, but remain unwilling to grow or evolve. That unwillingness is emotional immaturity, and it's not yours to carry.

This journal will walk you through the messy middle, the space between what hurts and what comes next. It will help you untangle the confusion, challenge the stories that kept you small, and rise into the version of yourself who no longer accepts anything less than genuine love and respect.

You are becoming, and this journal is your roadmap to your healing era.

What You'll Need.

A pen.

A quiet space.

21 minutes a day.

Start where you need.

Skip ahead if you want.

Come back when you're ready.

This space is *yours*.

The Rising Compass

A 21–DAY SYSTEM FOR EMOTIONAL WELLNESS & NERVOUS SYSTEM RESTORATION

This is your compass. A visual guide to how each tool in the journal supports your transformation, from daily rhythm to real–time resets, from micro–habits to mindset rewiring. Let this page ground you as you move through your healing, one layer at a time.

THE RISING COMPASS

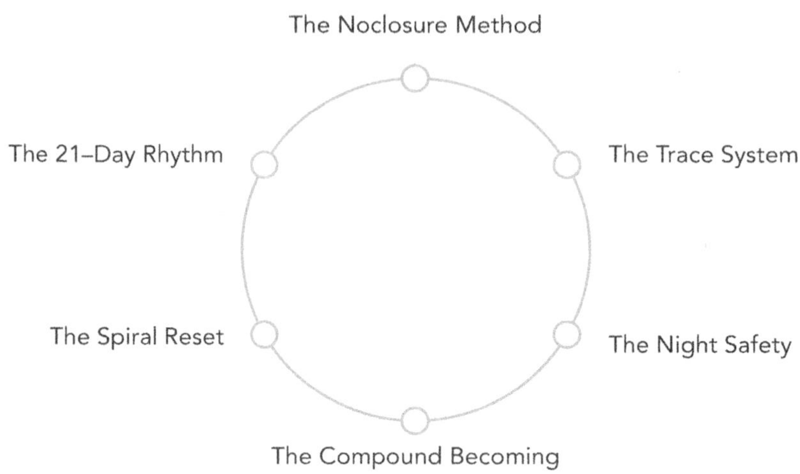

1

THE NOCLOSURE METHOD

21·7·7·7. Your core daily practice ritual: 7 min *Release* » 7 min *Reframe* » 7 min *Rewire*. Designed for deep rewiring.

2

THE 21 DAY RHYTHM

Your 21–day journey unfolds through three trauma–informed phases: Process · Build · Rise. Rooted in clarity and rhythm.

3

THE TRACE SYSTEM

Track emotional patterns and micro–boundaries to rebuild your nervous system baseline through awareness and boundaries.

4

THE SPIRAL RESET

A real–time nervous system regulation tool, for spirals, craving contact, or emotional overload.

5

THE NIGHT SAFETY

A three–step ritual to release the weight on your mind, restore clarity, and invite resolution when rest feels out of reach.

6

THE COMPOUND BECOMING

Where your healing becomes how you live, with tools to anchor growth into lasting embodiment.

The Noclosure Method 21·7·7·7

SCIENCE · MEETS · SOUL

The Noclosure Method

21·7·7·7

RELEASE · REFRAME · REWIRE

21 DAYS · 7 MINUTES · 7 MINUTES · 7 MINUTES

A rhythm for healing. A rhythm of safety. A Method designed for your nervous system to Release · Reframe · Rewire.

This is not a journal for venting. It's a structured space for repair, built on the neuroscience of emotional processing and the reality that unresolved pain doesn't fade with time. It needs intentional, repeated focus to begin rewiring how your brain responds to emotional pain, memory, and attachment. Built directly on the brain's natural architecture for emotional processing, it guides your nervous system through the exact sequence required for resolution: to *Release* what has not been integrated, *Reframe* the narrative with truth, and Rewire neural pathways with new safety.

The Science Behind 21 Days

When closure is denied, when words are left unsaid, explanations never given, or accountability never taken, your nervous system doesn't register the ending. It stays locked in survival mode, waiting for clarity and looping in search of resolution. But until that loop is closed, it can't fully let go. But here's what's understood from the science of healing:

It takes a minimum of 21 days of intentional, structured repetition to begin rewiring the brain's response to emotional pain, memory, and attachment.

This journal is built on that truth. *The Noclosure Method* gives your system what life withheld: a structured ending from the inside out—science-aligned, rhythm-based, and anchored in consistent practice. Each day walks you through a guided rhythm that helps your body *Release* what's heavy, *Reframe* what isn't yours to carry, and gently *Rewire* your patterns with clarity, intention, and deep self-compassion. In just 21 minutes a day, you'll move through the core emotional work of releasing, reframing, and rewiring—guided through three phases that support your healing journey, helping you *Process · Build · Rise.* And for that, you need a system.

How It Works:

21 DAYS	Because healing deserves science and rhythm.
THE PHASES	*3 phases (21 days)* *Process · Build · Rise*
THE METHOD	*3 daily steps (21 min)* *Release · Reframe · Rewire*
7 MINUTES EACH	the nervous system's sweet spot: enough to create impact, safe enough not to overwhelm.

The Daily Practice: 21·7·7·7

(21 minutes total)

Release *7 min*	Shed · Discharge
Reframe *7 min*	Shift · Perspective
Rewire *7 min*	Anchor · Wisdom

Each day, you move through the steps. Each week, you step into a new phase. Over 21 days, you will not just reflect, you will retrain your mind and body toward peace, strength, and self-trust.

Daily 21 Minutes: The 21·7·7·7 Method

You've seen the science and rhythm behind *The Noclosure Method.* Now, here's how it comes alive. In 21 minutes a day, you move through three steps: *Release · Reframe · Rewire.* Each lasts 7 minutes, aligned with the brain's natural rhythm for processing emotion. Rooted in neuroscience yet softened for the soul, this ritual helps you release what's heavy, reshape the story, and anchor safety as your new default. This is not journaling for reflection. It is structured closure, a rhythm that resolves what your body and mind could not close on their own. Over time, this rhythm becomes more than writing. It becomes a practice of rewiring—teaching your system a different ending, one that holds peace instead of pain. What follows is a ***preview*** of the rhythm you'll return to each day. The full 21–day journey will begin in Phase One.

Release what's heavy.	*Reframe the story.*	*Rewire with wisdom.*
7 min	*7 min*	*7 min*

Release *7 minutes of Emotional Release*

Supports the brain's capacity to discharge emotional weight. This step allows the unresolved ending to move through, releasing the loop so it no longer grips the body or mind.

"Write what feels unresolved. Let it leave the page."

Reframe *7 minutes of Cognitive Rewiring*

Engages the narrative where distortion once lived. By identifying limiting beliefs and reshaping the story, this step restores coherence, transforming confusion into clarity.

"What is the clearer truth here?"

Rewire *7 minutes of Anchoring the Reframe*

Leverages neuroplasticity to embed new patterns. Through wisdom and embodied clarity, this step anchors safety, boundaries, and truth as your system's default.

"What new ending do you want your body to remember?"

This rhythm is the heartbeat of Noclosure. Day by day, it rewires your system for resolution, teaching your body and mind to live in peace instead of pursuit.

The 3 Phases of Healing

ONE JOURNEY. THREE SEASONS OF BECOMING.

Over these 21 days, you'll journey through three intentional phases: *Process · Build · Rise*. Each is a season of becoming, designed to meet you where you are and carry you into who you are becoming. This arc isn't divided by weeks, but by emotional purpose. Every phase carries its own energy and evolution, reshaping your inner world. Healing here is not just loosening endings, but building the architecture of the self you are stepping into.

3 PHASES OF HEALING

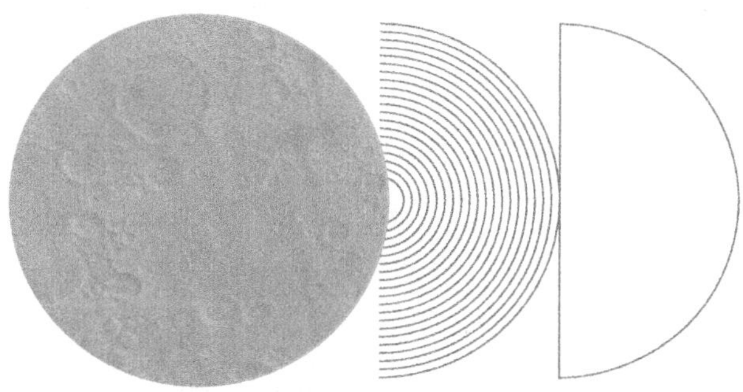

PHASE 1
PROCESS
(Days 1-7)

This is the season of *Processing*. The weight that once lingered begins to move through, and the nervous system exhales. With honesty and compassion, you release, clear space for clarity, and free your mind from the unfinished loops of the past.

PHASE 2
BUILD
(Days 8-14)

This is the season of *Rebuilding*. Old distortions soften and dissolve as you reshape the story with truth. You reclaim power through clarity, establish boundaries that honor your worth, and step into grounded self-trust.

PHASE 3
RISE
(Days 15-21)

This is the season of *Rise*. Survival softens into wisdom, and your ground strengthens. Anchored in safety and guided by clarity, you begin to live from a different lens, the quiet unfolding of your Becoming.

The Architecture of Becoming

This is the architecture of Becoming: three seasons woven into one journey of transformation. *Process* softens pain, *Build* restores strength, and *Rise* anchors wisdom. Together, they carry you from processing to creating, from clearing to building, from surviving into *Becoming*. What begins on these pages becomes daily practice. What begins as practice becomes the living architecture of your new self: grounded, integrated, and free.

21 minutes a day. Structured. Powerful. Science–aligned. Yours. A rhythm designed not just to help you cope, but to help you recalibrate.

—RISING JOURNEY

Trace System

This is not a checklist. It is a quiet recalibration of the nervous system. At the start of each seven-day phase, the Trace System grounds you in gentle, intentional habits that support healing. Trauma-informed and aligned with neuroscience, it functions as a ritual of self-relationship, guiding you to notice patterns, respect micro-boundaries, and subtly rewire how you move through life. Each habit marks a shift in thought, in behavior, in regulation. Seamlessly woven into *Process · Build · Rise.*

This work centers on alignment with your mind, your emotions, and your healing. It unfolds as rhythms you return to in each releasing ritual. The loop unwinds through consistency, clarity, and care. You are rebuilding boundaries and integrity with yourself through this process. One sacred habit at a time. One aligned decision each week. Over time, these habits become the foundation of your emotional baseline, rooted in self-trust, clarity, and strength.

How it works

Each phase: *Process · Build · Rise*—includes a 7-day tracker with five intentional micro-habits designed to support the emotional work of that stage. These are nervous system-safe actions: emotional habits, boundary shifts, and quiet moments of truth. Each aligned with that phase's specific focus-healing and *intention.*

- Choose 2–3 habits that resonate with your current season.
- After each releasing ritual, gently track the actions you honored, a reflection of your quiet devotion to healing.
- If you completed it, mark it with presence. If not, simply notice. Even the act of noticing is part of healing.

The tracker is yours to complete, reflect on, and return to as you grow. This is just a sample. Your full tracker will follow. Simple, intentional, and aligned with each phase of your healing.

HABITS	SUN	MON	TUE	WED	THU	FRI	SAT
1. Choose not to explain myself		✓	✓	✓			
2. No Contact			✓	✓	✓	✓	✓

Some days, healing looks like stillness. Like saying no. Like choosing rest instead of proving your worth. That counts, too.

Understanding *Noclosure*

Closure isn't always a conversation. Sometimes, it's the *realization* that no conversation would have ever been enough.

Noclosure is the specific grief that lives in the space between what was and what never got resolved. It's the emotional residue left behind when someone exits your life without taking responsibility for the damage they caused. It's the weight of unfinished business that your nervous system carries long after they've moved on. This shows up as questions that loop in your mind: Why did they change? What did I do wrong? How could they walk away? It's the way your body still tenses when you hear their name, how certain songs or places instantly flood you with memories and sadness. It's the confusion that lingers when someone who claimed to *care* about you could discard you so easily.

Noclosure happens in many forms

There are many ways a story can remain unfinished. Sometimes it's loud and shattering. Other times, it's silent and a door that never quite closed.

- The one who called you "the one," spoke of engagements, homes, and children, then pulled away when real commitment required them to show up.
- The partner who betrayed your trust but never acknowledged the betrayal, and left without ever looking back.
- The one who twisted the truth until you no longer trusted your own.
- The one who used your vulnerability against you, then told others you were the toxic one.

What makes a *Noclosure* so difficult is that it violates our fundamental need for understanding and completion. Your brain is wired to seek resolution, to make sense of experiences, and to process emotions fully.

When that natural cycle is interrupted by someone's inability or unwillingness to engage honestly, you're left with an open loop your mind keeps trying to close.

Noclosure is the ache of someone walking away. Not because love was missing, but because effort, growth, and responsibility were. You were willing to do the work. They weren't. And that's what hurts the most.

Here's the truth: their refusal to give you closure says nothing about your worth and everything about their capacity. People who can't handle accountability, difficult conversations, or emotional responsibility will always choose the easy exit. The one that requires the least of them, even if it causes significant harm to you.

This journal exists because you deserve better than their limitations. You deserve to find peace without their participation. You deserve to create your own ending to a story they abandoned halfway through.

Now that you understand what you're *healing* from, let's build the foundation for moving through it.

You do not have to chase, beg, or convince anyone to stay. You do not have to prove your worth to people who were never willing to see it. If someone walks away, let them go. That isn't abandonment it's redirection. If someone can't recognize your value, stop waiting for them to see it. If someone rewrites the past to avoid accountability, let them. You don't need to correct their version. You don't need their approval, their apology, or their permission to move on. This isn't about them anymore.

This is about you, your Healing, your Power, and your Freedom.

21 Lines I will Live By

REFLECTIONS THAT BECOME LIFE PRINCIPLES

This journal isn't about writing endlessly. It's about repetition that creates clarity and clarity that creates change. Each day, one prompt, one shift.

By the end of this journey, you'll carry 21 new *truths*. You'll notice certain insights return to the surface , your new standards. Not just reflections but Non–Negotiables—what you now believe, what you no longer tolerate, what you're finally choosing, and what you now live by.

Instead of letting those moments fade, you'll capture them, one sentence per day. One thought. One *pivotal* moment.

At the end of this journal, you'll find a space titled, *21 Lines I Will Live By*. These following 21 lines are yours and become your new standards. Write one per day or all at once, each one is a truth you *earned.*

21 Lines I Will Live By

1

2

Each one is a standard you now embody. Let this be your personal manifesto.

The Rhythm of Reset

YOU ARE NO LONGER WAITING FOR CLOSURE

Healing isn't only about letting go. It's about creating the right foundation, the right environment, and the proper structure for healing. This journal represents a shift in how you approach emotional wellness, with the same intention you bring to every other aspect of your life. Small rituals and small actions, done with intention, quietly compound over time, rebuilding your life from the inside out.

This journal is your space to *Process · Build · Rise*. Every page is a reminder that you are in control of your healing. From this moment on, you are not waiting. You are choosing. Choosing to move forward. Choosing to heal. This decision is not only a promise. It is a practice. Ahead, you will discover the rhythm your nervous system can trust. Because when there's no closure, the body doesn't know how to let go. It holds the tension, loops for meaning, and anticipates rupture that never arrives.

Healing is not only a shift in mindset. It is a full–body recalibration. Your nervous system doesn't heal through alone. It heals through rhythm, repetition, and safety. What follows are foundational Emotional Wellness Rituals, chosen with precision to guide your body out of survival and back into presence. These are new practices, new pathways, and invitations to rebuild what grief, betrayal, and abandonment left behind. Each one is structured and intentional, designed to regulate your system, restore peace, and help you feel safe again.

This is the structure your healing has been missing, a framework that reaches the root. When woven into your daily rhythm, these rituals become more than practices. They are anchors. They steady you, restore your balance, and quietly sustain your transformation.

Emotional Wellness Rituals

Healing is not an idea you think through. It is a rhythm you live through. Emotional wellness is built in the body, in the daily practices that signal safety, stability, and *clarity*. The rituals ahead meet your nervous system where survival once lived and begin to teach it peace. They offer a new language the body can learn to trust: stillness as *safety,* presence as strength. Each practice is small, intentional, and powerful, because healing does not arrive in a single moment. It *compounds,* action by action, day by day.

Each ritual is designed with precision to help your system release what it holds, guide you out of survival, and anchor you back into *presence*. They meet you where you are, support your return to clarity, and gently shift how your body carries pain, toward calm, steadiness, and peace. These practices are your anchors. They retrain your body to choose steadiness instead of reactivity, safety instead of hypervigilance, and clarity instead of confusion.

Journaling Method

Practice: Unprocessed stress will keep your system on alert. This isn't surface-level journaling. It's structured nervous system repair. *The Noclosure Method* was born from the places traditional healing left behind, that therapies logic couldn't soothe, the loops that clarity alone couldn't close. This is a 21-minute modern daily ritual grounded in neuroscience, rooted in compassion. It guides you through three trauma-informed steps: *Release,* to unburden the emotional weight, *Reframe,* to gently shift the lens, and *Rewire,* to imprint new internal safety. Each step mirrors the way the brain heals, not by rushing closure, but by slowly making space for peace. Light a candle. Sit where you feel safe. Let this practice become your daily return to peace and clarity, to feel, process, and rebuild from the inside.

21·7·7·7
Release · Reframe · Rewire
21 Days · 7 Minutes · 7 Minutes · 7 Minutes

Why this matters: Studies confirm that journaling rewires emotional pathways, soothes the amygdala, and helps integrate past experiences. But *The Noclosure Method* goes further. It transforms journaling into a trauma-aware rhythm, deliberately designed for nervous system healing. You're not just writing—you're releasing what's been trapped. You're not just reflecting—you're reframing what was distorted. You're not just remembering—you're rewiring your body with a new ending. One that isn't rushed, one that isn't forced, one that honors the mess, the truth, the time it takes. Over time, these 21 minutes become more than a practice. They become a soft transformation. One breath. One page. One rewiring at a time.

Together, these rituals reveal that journaling is not only writing on a page, but rewriting your nervous system, one breath, one page, one rewiring at a time.

Protect Your Energy

Practice: Boundaries are how you interrupt the patterns that once taught you to abandon yourself for the comfort of others. When you've lived in survival mode, your nervous system learned that love was earned by being everything to everyone, by shrinking, explaining, over-giving, and neglecting your own needs. But healing begins when you choose one boundary and hold it. Try:

- I don't need to reply right away.
- I don't need to explain myself.
- Not everyone gets access to me.

Why this matters: Each time you honor a boundary, you teach your mind that safety now comes from protecting your energy, not abandoning it. *Boundaries* create psychological safety and rebuild self-trust. Even one energetic boundary, held with intention, signals to your nervous system: You're safe now. You're in charge. You can trust yourself again.

Breathwork 4.4.4

Practice: Set a gentle alarm—midday, or whenever feels natural, as a cue for your healing breath. A quiet reminder to check in, pause, and breathe for 4 minutes. No distractions. Just you and your breath.

The 4·4·4 Rhythm:

- Inhale for 4 seconds
- Hold for 4 seconds
- Exhale for 4 seconds

Why it matters: When you've been living in survival mode, your breath turns shallow. Your body stays on guard. This daily pause tells your nervous system: you're safe now. It begins to unwind the tension that never had a chance to release. Over time, it becomes more than breathwork. It becomes a rhythm: Back to calm. Back to presence. Back to you. Each breath moves you from survival into restoration. After 21 days, you won't just be breathing, you'll feel yourself returning.

Attention Training Practice

Practice: At the heart of emotional regulation is the ability to sit with discomfort, witness emotion with steadiness, and allow it to move through—by staying present, breathing with it, and letting it complete its course. This is how energy shifts from rumination into regulation. When the brain feels rejection, silence, or uncertainty, it loops for resolution. That is why the same thoughts return again and again. This practice channels that energy differently: noticing the loop, and gently bringing attention back to the present, into breath, into body, into life. Instead of replaying conversations in search of answers, you choose to sit with what is here, move through it, and step to the other side. Each return to presence builds the capacity to remain, to regulate with steadiness, and to come back to yourself every single time.

Why this matters: The brain is wired to seek safety, even in painful stories that wound. Redirecting attention interrupts the cycle of rumination and begins creating new pathways. Each time you channel your energy into presence, you send a clear signal to your nervous system: safety is here. My attention belongs here, not there. With practice, the loop softens, presence deepens, and energy returns to you. The body learns a new truth: I can hold this. I am safe now. *Repeat this as often as you need.*

Morning Intention

Practice: Before reaching for your phone, place your hand over your heart and take three slow, grounding breaths. Whisper a clear *intention* for the day: "Today, I choose peace." "Today, I protect my energy." Then root yourself in a gentle truth: I am safe. I am healing. I am doing my best. So many beautiful things are on their way to me. Everything *unfolding* now is guiding me exactly where I'm meant to be. I am trusting the process.

Why this matters: The first moments of your day set the rhythm for your nervous system. When you begin with calm, clarity, and compassion, you teach your body to lead with safety, not urgency. You're no longer waking into survival. You're waking into intention.

She was left carrying more than she ever should have. Meet her with kindness. Meet her with compassion. That's how healing begins.

Mirror Talk

Practice: This is a quiet but profound nervous system ritual, one that restores inner safety, softens self-judgment, and helps you feel seen again. When doubt creeps in or old wounds resurface, meet your own eyes in the mirror.

Begin here, Look into your eyes:

- You are doing your best.
- You are *healing.*
- You are a wonderful soul.

Why this matters: Each time you do this, you begin to rewire the inner narrative that once kept you small. Instead of criticism, you offer love. Instead of threat, you offer safety. When you speak to yourself with compassion , especially while making eye contact, you activate your parasympathetic nervous system. Your body softens. Stress hormones lower. Heart rate variability rises. You begin to remember what it feels like to be safe within yourself. This is how you stop abandoning yourself. This is how you come home.

Inward Gratitude

Practice: This is a self-compassion gratitude ritual, a quiet moment to thank the part of you that kept going when it was hard to even breathe. Before falling asleep, close your eyes, place a hand over your heart, and take a slow, grounding breath. Bless the day for how it held you, and bless yourself for how you made it through. This isn't about the highlight moments. It's about the strength it took to keep going, and the *compassion* you offer yourself for getting through it. It's about honoring the part of you no one else saw. The part that carried the pain, held the broken pieces, and still chose to *rise.* Name three things you are grateful for: in yourself, for your resilience, your courage, your breath; and in the world around you, for whatever held you today. Even if all you can say is: "I made it through today." Then pause. Thank the day for its small mercies. And thank yourself, for enduring, for *surviving,* for being here.

Why this matters: When gratitude is reframed toward the self, it becomes a practice of deep love. It strengthens the part of you that no longer accepts what once harmed you. Gratitude steadies the nervous system. Compassion softens the inner critic. And repetition turns into sanctuary. A daily reminder that beauty still lives here, even in the midst of healing.

“When we are no longer able to change a situation, we are challenged to change ourselves.”

VIKTOR E. FRANKL

The Commitment Contract

This is not just a journal. This is a decision. A decision to move forward. To stop waiting for closure and create your own. For the next 21 days, you are making a sacred commitment to yourself. Whether you are releasing a toxic relationship, moving on from a divorce, healing from narcissistic abuse, or shedding years of emotional weight, this is it.

You are choosing to show up.
To feel. To reflect. To shift. To *rise*.
Write clearly and honestly.

What I Am Leaving Behind:

What I Am Moving Toward:

My Promise to Myself:

I promise to show up consistently for 21 days. I promise to honor my healing. I promise to no longer abandon myself for the comfort of others. I promise to finish this journey stronger, softer, and free. By signing below, I make this sacred commitment to myself.

Date: .... Signature: ....

Before We Continue

A MOMENT OF TRUTH

You've made your commitment to healing. You've identified what you're leaving behind and what you're moving toward. Now comes the part that may feel uncomfortable, but it is the most important one.

Your gut already knows.

Deep down, you already know what's been keeping you stuck. You know which relationships drain your energy. Which conversations leave you feeling worse, not better. You know when someone's presence—even digitally, pulls you backward instead of forward. And your nervous system knows it too.

Sometimes we stay in loops, telling ourselves we're being kind, mature, or diplomatic. But really, we've been overriding what the body has been whispering all along: this is not safe. And until you name that truth, your nervous system cannot exhale.

The choice is yours. It always has been. But if you are truly ready to heal. If you are serious about moving forward, if you are done recycling the same pain over and over again. Then you already know what needs to happen.

For most, the right choice is No Contact. Not because it is easy. Because it works. *In some situations, such as shared responsibilities or co-parenting, no contact may need to be adapted. The intention remains the same: clear boundaries, minimal communication, and emotional disengagement beyond what is required.*

Your healing depends on it. Your peace requires it. Your future self is counting on it.

You are Protecting Your *Space*. Protecting Your *Peace*. Protecting Your *Progress*.

The choice is yours.

The No Contact Contract

You've listened to your intuition. You've acknowledged the truth. Now it's time to make it official. Healing cannot happen while old wounds are constantly reopened. Freedom cannot grow where toxic ties remain. You already know this. *Now you're ready to act on it.*

BY SIGNING THIS NO CONTACT CONTRACT, I COMMIT TO:

1. *Ending all communication with the person, people, or situation that caused harm.*
2. *Blocking, deleting, or removing access from all platforms (phone, social media, email).*
3. *Refusing to seek updates, indirect contact, or third-party information about them.*
4. *Redirecting my focus entirely to my healing, my growth, and my future.*

I understand that breaking no contact is not just a relapse, it is a *delay* in my healing. I am no longer available for false hope, emotional confusion, or recycled pain. I choose clarity. I choose peace. I choose myself.

The No Contact Starts Today

I commit to 21 days minimum of complete no contact. No calls, texts, emails, or social media interaction.

- Blocking or muting them on all platforms—phone, social media, dating apps.
- No asking mutual friends for updates about how they're doing or what they're up to.
- When the urge to contact them arises, return first to your Reality Check (next page) or your Illusion Breaker (end of Phase 1 section).
- Build a support system: have at least one safe friend you can lean on or vent to.

This is protection. This is clarity. This is strength. This is your truth. You already carry the knowing. Now choose to live it.

Date: .... Signature: ....

You honor your worth each time you don't reach out. Each time you stop yourself from calling, from explaining, from chasing. You reclaim your power in the pause, when you take a breath and ask, 'What do I need right now?' That moment is everything. It says:

I'm done proving myself to someone who only showed up when it was convenient for them.

Honor this commitment before moving forward to Phase 1.

Reality Check

When You Want to Go Back: *Remember This*

There will be moments when your heart forgets. When the pain softens just enough for nostalgia to creep in. When you remember their laugh, their touch, the way they made you feel in the beginning.

WHEN YOU WANT TO GO BACK, REMEMBER THIS:

How did they make you feel about yourself in the hardest moments?

What they said or did that broke you:

How they made you feel about yourself:

The times you begged for basic respect:

How your body felt around them toward the end:

Read this when you miss them.
Read this when you think about calling.
Read this when you wonder if you made a mistake.
You didn't leave because you stopped loving them.
You left because you finally chose yourself.
Don't go back to a place that required you to lose your authentic self.
Don't return to someone who genuinely hurt you.
Don't trade your peace for their temporary comfort.
Don't sacrifice your healing for a temporary emotion.
When you miss them, you are not remembering the whole truth,
you are remembering selectively.

Come back here whenever your heart tries to rewrite history.

REMINDER

If you need more space, use this page. Write the truths, the details, the things left unsaid. The reality of how they showed up. This is your reminder: don't erase what happened, but release what you no longer need to carry.

You're not still thinking about them because they were your person. You're thinking about them because your nervous system hasn't caught up to your reality yet.
Watching their life from afar doesn't bring closure, it keeps you stuck in a version of your life that no longer exists.

The more you check in on their world, the more you disconnect from your own.

You have to stop rehearsing the past to make space for what's next.

This is protection. This is redirection. This is your healing.

The Practice of Allowing

YOUR ANCHOR

"Peace begins the moment you stop reaching back toward what broke you."

Allowing is the soul of *Release · Reframe · Rewire.* Releasing the ache of begging for love where it was withheld, reframing silence not as abandonment but as truth revealed, and rewiring your body to trust life's order over the illusions of longing. To allow is to live without pursuit or persuasion, to let life place into your hands what is meant for you and dissolve what is not. It is to rise anchored in such worth that you no longer beg to be chosen, but rest instead in clarity, trust, and becoming.

The Practice of Allowing

For the next 21 days, your mind may try to pull you back. You may feel the urge to check their social media, to send a message, or to replay conversations that will never bring peace. Pause. Breathe. That is not your path anymore.

Allowing is the quiet decision to no longer chase, explain, or correct. It is the art of stepping back and letting people reveal who they are. Without chasing clarity, defending your truth, or resisting what unfolds, you reclaim your peace. It is not about letting go in anger, but about stepping back in self-respect, a boundary that says: I choose peace over proving.

Allowing is both *biology* and *courage.* On a nervous system level, it interrupts the survival loop that circles the past, teaching the body to settle into safety. On a soul level, it is surrender. Trusting that what is aligned will remain, and what is misaligned will gently dissolve. Here, science and spirit converge: the mind exhales, the heart rests, and peace takes root.

The Allowing Sequence

- Allow them to misunderstand your silence.
- Allow them to rewrite the story to protect their ego.
- Allow them to choose someone else.
- Allow them to reveal who they are, and believe their actions more than their words.

You are no longer here to beg anyone to be with you. You are no longer here to convince anyone of your value. You are no longer available for confusion disguised as a connection.

Whatever your past has been, whatever your story holds, you now stand at the edge of something new. To step into it, you release what is behind you, with quiet trust in your path forward, and with the knowing that you deserve love far greater than the pain you've carried.

"What's meant for you will find you.
Even across lifetimes, mountains, and oceans,
it will make its way to you.
Trust the process. Heal.
Become ready for what's already written.
The universe has got you.
And so many beautiful things are already on
their way."

—RISING JOURNEY

You've set your commitment. You've cleared space. You've created emotional safety.

Now, it's time to begin your healing. Over the next 21 days, you'll move through three core phases: *Process · Build · Rise.*

Each day follows a rhythm: a journaling prompt to *Release,* a mindset shift to *Reframe,* and an integration to *Rewire* your nervous system. This is *The 21·7·7·7 Method*—a structured, trauma-informed practice for deep emotional healing in just 21 minutes a day.

Your only role now is to arrive, gently, consistently, and with intention. The rest will unfold from there.

This is more than a journal. It's a structure for true transformation, and through each intentional phase, becoming unfolds.

PHASE 1
PROCESS

DAYS 1–7 | PROCESSING NOCLOSURE

You were left without closure. This is where you begin anyway. They walked away—or maybe they stayed but disappeared emotionally. There was no apology. No accountability. No real goodbye. Just silence, confusion, and pain you never asked to carry. You had good intentions. You waited, you *loved,* hoping they would take responsibility, grow, or even just understand. But they didn't. And now, you stop waiting for what never came.

This phase is about facing the truth. It's the moment you recognize that some relationships were never the right fit. You stop romanticizing what never was, and you stop minimizing what actually happened. Instead of pouring energy into what cannot change, you rechannel it back into yourself. Into healing, into clarity, into the life already waiting for *you.*

In this phase:

- You name what happened.
- You face what is real.
- You process the emotions and patterns.
- You rewire the story into truth.

It's where the wound meets the light. It's about releasing. It's about processing. It's about feeling, letting the pain move through. Healing begins here: in the honesty of what hurts, in the courage to face it, and in the choice to finally let it shift.

This is your goodbye. This is your closure. Even if they never gave you one.

If at any given time this feels overwhelming, give yourself permission to stop and take a grounding breath.

TRACE SYSTEM

Weekly Intention Prompt:

This week, I am releasing: ....

This week's habits are about clearing emotional baggage and reclaiming peace. Choose 3–4 practices from the. List—or create your own—that feel aligned with where you are in this phase. After journaling each day, gently track your actions as a quiet commitment to your healing.

Intention

This week is about processing what's kept you in survival and rebuilding your emotional foundation. Let go of guilt, over-explaining, and the need to be understood. You're wise for choosing peace.

Micro-Habits to Choose From

Choose 1 to 3. Track 1 or 2 daily.

- Didn't reach out to seek closure
- Reminded myself: "Their silence is not my worth"
- Resisted checking their social media
- Deleted a trigger (memory, photo, gift)
- Went no contact
- Replaced fantasy with truth (e.g., return to your Reality Check or Illusion Breaker)

HABITS	SUN	MON	TUE	WED	THU	FRI	SAT
	☐	☐	☐	☐	☐	☐	☐
	☐	☐	☐	☐	☐	☐	☐
	☐	☐	☐	☐	☐	☐	☐
	☐	☐	☐	☐	☐	☐	☐
	☐	☐	☐	☐	☐	☐	☐
	☐	☐	☐	☐	☐	☐	☐

One aligned habit. One soft release. This is how your nervous system learns to feel safe again.

Let it hurt.
Let it heal.
Let it go.

—R.H. Sin

Day 1 — Radical Honesty

Release *.7 min*

What was I really hoping for in this relationship that I did not receive? Financial security, emotional safety, status, attention, validation, or relief from the fear of being alone. Allow the emotional truth to surface as it is, including the parts that feel difficult to admit.

Reframe *.7 min*

It is strength to admit your needs were not met, because that admission is the beginning of self-trust. Breaking the belief that kept you stuck opens the door to a new lens: unmet needs are not shameful. They are signals, guiding you toward the patterns, the wounds, and the places within you that are ready to be healed.

Rewire *.7 min*

I see my unmet needs as teachers, not failures. They show me where I need to grow and heal. This is the anchor. Let it land. A quiet decision to face myself with compassion and do the inner work.

Day 2 — Detachment from Fantasy

Release *.7 min*

What person did I make up in my head that was completely different from who they actually showed me? Get specific: Did I make them more emotionally available? More committed? More capable of love? What behaviors did I excuse or rewrite? What harsh truths did I soften into romantic stories? Write down the gap between who they were and who I needed them to be.

Reframe *.7 min*

Your intuition was never wrong, only waiting for you to listen. *Your nervous system was collecting evidence while your heart was editing the story.* You really wanted this relationship to work, so you diminished reality and upgraded who they weren't. But now you know better. Break this belief: that hope means ignoring red flags. New lens: Your body knew what your mind wasn't ready to accept. Those warnings weren't obstacles. They were protection.

Rewire *.7 min*

I trust my intuition over the stories my mind once told. I no longer rewrite someone's actions to make them easier to love. My peace is sacred and it is no longer up for negotiation.

You never have to chase, beg, or persuade anyone to stay.
You never have to prove your worth to those unwilling to see it.
If someone walks away, allow them to go—that is not abandonment, it is path redirection.
If someone cannot recognize your value, stop waiting for them to see it. Your worth was never theirs to define. Allow life to unfold as it must.
If someone rewrites the past to escape accountability, allow the universe to hold the truth. What is meant for you will never require convincing.
You do not need to correct their version.
You do not need their approval, their apology, or their permission to move on.
This is no longer about them.
This is about you. Your healing, your power, your freedom.

Day 3 — Self-Forgiveness

Release *.7 min*

In what ways did I abandon myself to stay connected? Did I silence my voice when they dismissed me, ignore my boundaries when they crossed them, minimize my needs to avoid conflict, or betray my values to keep their attention? What parts of myself did I sacrifice, suppress, or compromise? Write down every way you made yourself smaller to make them stay.

Reframe *.7 min*

You weren't trying to save the relationship—you were trying to save yourself from the fear of being alone. Self-abandonment felt safer than potential rejection. Break this belief: that love requires you to silence your truth. New lens: You abandoned yourself because you didn't trust that the real you was worth choosing. This wasn't love, it was self-betrayal disguised as love.

Rewire *.7 min*

I forgive myself fully and reclaim every part of me I once silenced to stay. I forgive myself for the ways I abandoned my own truth. My authentic voice matters more than maintaining false peace. I will no longer diminish or lower myself to fit into spaces that reject or disrespect the real me. Feel the weight leaving your body. This is reclamation.

Day 4 — The Red Flags I Ignored

Release *.7 min*

The moments your gut knew something was wrong, but you found reasons to ignore it. What red flags did I recognize and dismiss and why? Was it in the name of hope, potential, or who I wanted them to be? What will I choose differently moving forward? What patterns will I no longer justify, and what behaviors will I no longer tolerate moving forward?

Reframe *.7 min*

Red flags don't arrive to ruin connection, they arrive to protect you. *Your nervous system noticed what your heart wasn't ready to accept.* Ignoring the signs was hope, paired with good intentions. *Break this belief:* That recognizing red flags means you're sabotaging something promising, or that naming what feels off makes you difficult. *New lens:* You weren't wrong for seeing potential—you were hopeful and open-hearted. But real love doesn't live in what could be; it reveals itself in what consistently is. Trusting your instinct isn't losing love, it's choosing alignment. The right connection won't ask you to explain away your standards. It will feel mutual, peaceful, and safe.

Rewire *.7 min*

I no longer override my intuition. I trust the warning signs. Staying hopeful at the cost of my peace is a pattern I'm no longer repeating. This time, I believe myself the first time.

Day 5 — What Your Body Remembers

Release *.7 min*

What routines, feelings, or reflexes from this relationship are still living in me? Do I still reach for my phone to text them, feel their absence in certain spaces, or forget for a moment that they are gone? What habits or responses am I still carrying that were shaped by being with them? Write down the ways my body is adjusting to this new reality.

Reframe *.7 min*

Your body remembers love, it's not weakness, it's proof of how deeply you loved. Missing someone after sharing space, time, and intimacy is not a sign to return. It's a natural response to loss. *Break this belief:* that missing them means you should go back. *New lens:* Your body is processing a real loss. Grief lives in the body, and real healing requires going through the pain, not around it. You're human, and you are healing. one day at a time.

Rewire *.7 min*

My body is learning a new normal without them. I honor the love it remembers, but I no longer mistake it as a reason to return. Missing them is not a call to go back. I allow myself to grieve, to heal, and to reclaim the space within me. With each day, my nervous system relearns safety, steadiness, and the truth that I am whole on my own.

Day 6 — What You Thought You Needed

Release *.7 min*

What did I believe they were "bringing to the table" that I could not give myself? Be specific: financial security, protection, direction, validation, social status, a sense of purpose? What qualities did I place on a pedestal in them while ignoring or underdeveloping those qualities in myself? Where did I hand them the role of being the source of something I didn't yet know how to create? Write it all down. Then, for each one, write a plan: If I was seeking it from them, it means I need to build it for myself now. How will I create financial security? How will I provide myself with protection, direction, validation, or purpose? This is the work. To take back what I thought I could only receive through them and make it mine.

Reframe *.7 min*

You didn't need them to be whole. You convinced yourself you were incomplete to justify staying. Wanting support isn't weakness. Yet the shortcut of leaning on someone else can't replace the deeper work. Break this belief: that someone else holds the key to your worth, safety, or happiness or to anything they seemed to provide. New lens: you outsourced your needs because you didn't trust you were capable of creating what you needed. What you admired in them was only a reflection of what you were seeking, the very things waiting to be built within yourself.

Rewire *.7 min*

I reclaim every quality I once projected onto them as my own. I am my own source of safety, direction, and worth. Whatever I was seeking in them, I now choose to create within myself—without compromise, without cost to my peace. This is where I begin showing up for myself, my mindset, and my growth in the ways I once waited for.

The wound was never your fault. But the work of processing and healing cannot belong to anyone else. It belongs to you. Your peace depends on it. So does the story of your next chapter, and the love you will one day allow.

Day 7 — Conscious Closure

Release *.7 min*

What am I ready to leave behind, and who am I choosing to become? What hope am I done carrying? What beliefs about love, worth, or relationships no longer serve me? What patterns am I releasing forever? What part of this experience am I ready to declare finished for good? This is your final accounting. Write down everything you are closing the door on, once and for all.

Reframe *.7 min*

Closure isn't about understanding why they hurt you, it's about accepting that they did. People will not change because you want them to, and waiting for them only keeps you bleeding from wounds they will never heal. Break this belief: that closure requires another conversation, their participation, or an explanation. New lens: some chapters simply end, and that is still an ending. You don't need a perfect goodbye to have a complete one.

Rewire *.7 min*

I allow what has been to rest, and I trust the path unfolding ahead. What is meant for me will not pass me by. With each step forward, I heal, I build, and I evolve into my highest self.

Letter to Me

Dear Past Self,

I'm so sorry you had to carry so much. You gave your love, the deepest, most innocent parts of yourself, to someone who never knew how to hold them. You placed your heart in their hands, hoping they'd protect it. You whispered your truth, praying they'd hear you. But they didn't. And still... you stayed. Not because you were weak, but because you loved with everything you had. Wanting to be chosen was never something to be ashamed of.

I see how many nights you stayed up wondering what more you could've done. How many times you silenced your needs, softened your truth, and bent yourself into someone more lovable just to keep the connection alive. But love that asks you to abandon yourself isn't love. Their inability to meet you was never your failure. You believed in love, and that belief made you beautiful. Even when it broke you, you kept loving. I honor every version of you that was left unseen.

Your love was true. Your hope was pure. You simply saw the best in someone who couldn't meet you there. But their limitations were never your burden. Their avoidance was never your responsibility. And their inability to choose you had nothing to do with your value. Today, I Release the pain you've carried. You didn't fail, you were simply trying to make a home out of something that was never safe.

So now, I take your hand with love. I promise to never abandon you again. I will no longer shrink to be chosen, or silence myself to feel loved. The version of me you've protected all this time is ready to rise. And this time, she will choose herself. One boundary at a time, one truth at a time, one breath at a time. I love you. I forgive you. And I'm so proud of how far you've come.

Signature: ....

End of Week 1 Reflection

PROCESS

THEME | RELEASING WHAT NO LONGER SERVES YOU

What old belief or story began to shift this week?

- *Maybe it was the belief that you had to hold it all together to be loved.*
- *Or the story that their behavior was your responsibility to fix.*

What boundary did I begin to practice or recognize I need?

- *Did you begin saying no—even if it felt uncomfortable?*
- *Or realize silence is also a boundary?*

What am I proud of myself for this week, no matter how small?

- *Getting out of bed on a heavy morning.*
- *Choosing not to reply.*

Mini Grounding Reminder:

You had the courage to face what most people avoid. Every truth you named, every feeling you allowed, every moment you chose honesty over denial—that's brave work. You're already healing. You've now completed a full week of *The 21·7·7·7 Method* and your system is already starting to shift.

Every day you show up, you're building the kind of self–trust that doesn't just heal... it Rewires.

A chapter has ended.
A test has passed.
A lesson has been learned.
A karmic bond has been broken.
And now, it is time to grow again.
With stronger roots.
With cleaner wings.
With a heart that remembers:
It was never her lack.
It was their limitation
to meet the depth of her love.

—RISING JOURNEY

Spiral Reset

Breakup grief without closure creates the most painful loop of all: mental rumination, the endless need to understand why, the overthinking of what was never said. This Reset was created to calm your nervous system, interrupt the spiral, and give your mind what it craves most: a sense of emotional resolution. You didn't get the ending you deserved, but now, you can give your mind a place to land every time the loop begins again. This is more than a journal tool—it's a healing companion. A nervous system framework. A daily return. And soon, it will speak back—a rising, emotionally trained system, revolutionized to guide you through the spiral in real time. Grounding. Human. Rooted in emotional science. Built for what therapy often can't hold—the urgency of the moment. Now pause. ***Breathe again. Pause. Count: 1 · 2 · 3 · 4 · 5 · 6.***

1. Breathe | *2. Name* | *3. Stop* | *4. Forgive* | *5. Live* | *6. Anchor*

1. BREATHE

This is your reset. A moment to interrupt the spiral and signal safety to your nervous system. Hand over heart. Breathe: *Inhale (4) · Hold (4) · Exhale (4)— repeat x3* Let your breath say: "I'm safe. I'm feeling. I'm healing." Breathe again. Pause. Count: 1 · 2 · 3 · 4 · 5 · 6 —and begin again.

2. NAME

You don't need to protect the past with hope anymore. It may have been unbalanced, emotionally unsafe, or manipulative. Maybe it wasn't love, maybe it was control, confusion, or inconsistency. Naming the truth ends the illusion.

3. STOP

This is the moment to choose peace over obsession. You don't need another explanation. You don't need another conversation, because you now understand: some people will never meet you with the integrity or accountability you deserve. *Wish them well.* Let the universe handle the rest, because it always does.

4. FORGIVE

You stayed because you loved. You tried because you believed. But now you know better, and that knowing is enough. Forgiveness doesn't mean forgetting—it means freeing yourself from the need to understand. because life's already handling it.

5. LIVE

You are not rebuilding the old version of yourself. You are becoming someone softer, stronger, more whole. When the thoughts come, let them pass. Do not react, do not engage. Gently rechannel your energy into living, into feeling, into fully being in this moment.

6. ANCHOR

End with a nervous system anchor:
Place a hand on your heart and say:
"I'm safe. I'm living. I'm healing. I'm evolving"
then Choose a micro-action: drink water, step outside, stretch—then re-enter your day with softness.

Healing isn't a straight line. When the waves rise again, this reset will meet you in real time, helping you pause, breathe, and gently reset the spiral.

Illusion Breaker

Purpose: Because the version you miss isn't the one that stayed. To separate the image of who you wished they were from the truth of who they have consistently shown themselves to be. This clarity interrupts the emotional loop that fuels longing, romanticizes the past, and keeps you waiting for closure. Seeing the gap between the version you hoped for and the reality you experienced makes the fantasy lose its pull. This is not about erasing the good, but about seeing it alongside the full truth.

Step 2 —Pattern Spotting: Circle the words or behaviors that repeat in the Reality column. Notice how many are missing from the Fantasy column. This is where the gap lies, and this gap is what keeps you stuck.

FANTASY

The version you wish existed, the idealized role they played at the beginning. Write about the loving, caring, consistent partner you wanted them to be. Include good moments, even the ones you romanticized.

REALITY

The person they have shown me they truly are, revealed through repeated patterns, actions, and choices, is their actual, consistent capacity for love, care, honesty, and reliability once the mask has fallen.

ANCHORING STATEMENT

Keep this page accessible and re-read it whenever hope resurfaces. The goal isn't to erase the good memories, but to see them in their true context so they stop pulling you back into the cycle.

PHASE 2

BUILD

DAYS 8–14 | FROM PROCESS TO BUILD

You've named the truth. You've felt the pain. Now comes the shift. This phase is about more than healing, it's about rebuilding. You're no longer focused on what hurt you. You begin to see the patterns, and a bigger picture starts to form around your healing and becoming.

In this phase:

You start to reprogram how you think, how you love, and what you allow. This is where the work deepens—where real realization begins. You identify the patterns you once couldn't see. You challenge the beliefs that made toxic feel like love. You raise your standards for how you deserve to be treated, and you begin showing up for yourself the way you always hoped someone else would. This ensures you don't just move on, you move forward *differently.*

You're not erasing your story. You're closing a chapter wiser and with clarity.

Let the rebuilding begin.

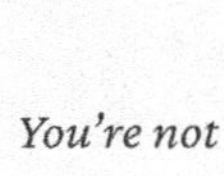

If at any given time this feels overwhelming, give yourself permission to stop and take a grounding breath.

TRACE SYSTEM

WEEKLY INTENTION PROMPT:

This week, I commit to .... even if it makes others uncomfortable.

You've cleared space by letting go. Now it's time to *Build* trust with your voice and your needs. This is the quiet work of practicing boundaries, a way to honor your growth and reconnect with your inner self. Choose or create 3–4 habits that feel true to you this week. After journaling each day, gently track what you honored, a reflection of presence, not performance.

Intention

Every pause, every truth spoken, every limit honored is part of the rewiring. This is how you begin to live differently. Each aligned choice, quiet boundary, and moment of self-honesty becomes part of your new rhythm, where healing leads.

Micro-Habits to Choose From

Choose 1 to 3. Track 1 or 2 daily.

- Held a boundary
- Didn't respond when triggered
- Resisted the urge to explain myself
- Didn't check (their name, profile, or chat)
- Blocked for peace
- Paused before reacting

HABITS	SUN	MON	TUE	WED	THU	FRI	SAT

One gentle action each day. One aligned decision at a time.

Day 8 — Not Everything Is Yours to Carry

Release *.7 min*

What burdens or roles did I take on in this relationship that were never mine to carry? Did I become their financial support, their emotional regulator, or the one who fixed their problems while ignoring my own? Did I take responsibility for their moods, reactions, or choices? What did I carry that actually belonged to them? List every way I became responsible for what was never my responsibility.

Reframe *.7 min*

Just because you were willing to fix it all doesn't mean it was your responsibility. Overgiving is not love. It is a trauma response disguised as devotion. You carried their weight to feel needed, not to feel loved. *Break this belief:* that your worth is measured by how much you can give or endure for others. *New lens:* Love does not ask you to be a savior. Healthy relationships honor balance, mutual responsibility, and care.

Rewire *.7 min*

I return what was never mine to carry. I am no longer the fixer, savior, or emotional container for others' wounds. My worth isn't measured by what I sacrifice for others.

Day 9 — The Stories I Inherited

Release *.7 min*

Conflict, carrying their weight, or giving more than we received. These patterns often come from old lessons—childhood, past relationships, or culture—that taught us love must be earned through sacrifice. Where did I abandon my needs, my voice, or my truth to keep the connection? Write down the moments I carried what was never mine. Then ask: What did I fear would happen if I spoke up or said no? What part of me was I protecting by staying small? What was the cost of disappearing? And what am I ready to release so I no longer confuse sacrifice with love?

Reframe *.7 min*

Most of your beliefs about love weren't truly yours—they were shaped by people doing their best, even if they were still carrying unhealed wounds. You've been living inside someone else's definition of love. Not your own. *Break this belief:* That these patterns are simply who you are. *New lens:* Every story that doesn't serve you can be rewritten. The cycle ends with you. You are no longer repeating, you're remembering, and you are learning. You now have the wisdom to choose differently. More educated. More aware. More whole.

Rewire *.7 min*

I break the patterns. I release what isn't mine. I open myself to love that is safe, mutual, and rooted in respect. I choose relationships that meet me with the same care I offer.

Day 10 — Boundaries Are Not Walls

Release *.7 min*

Where did I ignore my boundaries to stay in connection? Get specific: What behaviors did I tolerate that made me uncomfortable? When did I say yes when I meant no? What lines did I let them cross repeatedly? What requests did I agree to that violated my values? What treatment did I accept that I'd never accept from a friend? Where did I abandon myself to preserve the relationship? List every boundary you compromised and what it cost you.

Reframe *.7 min*

You confused love with accommodation, believing that having boundaries and needs made you difficult. *Break this belief:* that boundaries push good people away. Boundaries don't push love away—they protect your peace and reveal who's truly capable of loving you and staying. *New lens:* People who respect you will respect your limits. Those who don't were never meant to stay.

Rewire *.7 min*

My boundaries are non-negotiable acts of self-love. I protect my peace without guilt or explanation. The right people meet my limits with understanding and care.

Day 11 — Redefining What Love Looks Like

Release *.7 min*

What behaviors did I accept as love that were actually rooted in control, instability, or emotional neglect? Did I mistake jealousy for care, silence for boundaries, or control for protection? What did I normalize that felt like love but quietly fractured my sense of self?

Reframe *.7 min*

You've been moving through love with a definition shaped by survival, not self-awareness. What felt like passion was often unprocessed pain. What seemed like mystery was simply emotional instability. Through a clearer lens, instability is no longer mistaken for depth, and healthy love is no longer misunderstood as something lacking. Real love is steady, attuned, and safe. It meets you in your wholeness and grows without performance.

Rewire *.7 min*

I redefine love as peace, consistency, and mutual respect. The kind that feels safe, steady, and nourishing. I'm no longer available for anything less.

Day 12 — Emotional Needs

Release *.7 min*

How can I show up for my emotional needs in the ways I once wished they would? When I'm sad, what comfort do I need? When I'm anxious, what reassurance helps me feel safe? When I'm celebrating, how do I want to be acknowledged? What emotional support did I crave from them, and how can I begin offering that to myself? In what ways can I become my own safe sanctuary? Find them and write them down.

Reframe *.7 min*

The emotional availability you longed for begins within. Every time you dismissed your sadness, minimized your anxiety, or told yourself "it's all good," you were teaching your nervous system and the people around you how to treat you and that your feelings were optional. When you stop betraying your own emotions, you stop tolerating relationships that echo that same neglect. *Break this belief:* that your emotional needs are secondary. *New lens:* the way you soothe, comfort, and stand by your feelings becomes the standard. It shows others how to love you with the same presence you now give yourself.

Rewire *.7 min*

I am emotionally present with myself. I validate my feelings, meet my needs, and create the safety I once sought from others.

Day 13 — Love vs. Attachment

Release *.7 min*

Sometimes we accept fear, control, or attachment and call it love. Confusing possessiveness with care, anxiety with connection, or the need to be needed with being loved. Think of the moments where this showed up in your life. What did it give you in the moment—safety, attention, belonging? What did it cost you over time—your peace, your trust, your voice? How did your body learn to mistake intensity for intimacy? And what would it look like now to let love feel safe, steady, and free instead of anxious and consuming? Write it out so you can see the pattern clearly and begin choosing differently.

Reframe *.7 min*

Attachment can feel like love, but real love doesn't make you abandon yourself or question your worth when someone pulls away. You were conditioned to crave intensity, to confuse emotional highs with connection, and instability with depth. *Break this belief:* That the most intense emotions always reflect the deepest love. *New lens:* Real love is rooted in safety. It brings clarity, peace, and growth. It strengthens your sense of self. Attachment may look like love, but it's often unmet needs dressed as devotion.

Rewire *.7 min*

I recognize the difference between love and attachment. I choose what feels steady, sincere, and soul–honoring. I welcome the kind of love that feels like truth, and release the belief that intensity and high chemistry ever defined real love.

Day 14 — The New Standard

Release *.7 min*

What is my new standard for love, connection, and self-respect moving forward? What behaviors will I no longer tolerate? What treatment do I now require? What qualities must I intentionally scan for in a new partner, and which are non-negotiable? What red flags will I trust the first time they appear? What does respect look like in action, not just words?

Reframe *.7 min*

Your standards aren't too much—they are a reflection of your self-worth and a quiet protector of your peace. Somewhere along the way, you were made to believe that having requirements made you difficult, that knowing what you need was something to apologize for. *Break this belief:* that high standards make you unlovable or hard to be with. *New lens:* Standards don't push love away, they attract those capable of meeting you where you are. The right person will see your boundaries as strength, and your standards as self-respect.

Rewire *.7 min*

I don't lower my standards to be chosen. I hold them high and trust that aligned love will meet me there. My standards protect what I've built and honor who I've become.

The Relationship Standard

In Day 14, you've named your new standards—what you will no longer tolerate, what treatment you now require, and the qualities that are non-negotiable. The next step is to anchor them. Healing from *Noclosure* brings clarity, wisdom and direction. The path forward means recognizing red flags with precision and choosing to respond differently, rewriting the story of love itself. Non-negotiables are not preferences. They are protections. They safeguard against old wounds while creating space for growth, safety, and steady connection. Declaring these standards as life non-negotiables imprints them into the subconscious, teaching the nervous system what *love* must feel like, *grounded, consistent,* and *respectful.* From this place, the Relationship Standard emerges: a clear declaration of what will no longer be tolerated, the treatment that is now required, the qualities that are non-negotiable, and the red flags that will be recognized the first time they appear.

Non Negotiable Qualities to Scan for in a New Partner

EMOTIONAL AVAILABILITY

They remain present in conflict and open to real communication, instead of shutting down, disappearing, or stonewalling.

KINDNESS UNDER STRESS

It's easy to be kind when life is smooth. True character is shown in how they treat you under pressure, disappointment, or anger.

CONSISTENCY

Their words and actions align over time. No cycles of intensity followed by withdrawal. Consistency builds trust.

SUPPORT FOR GROWTH

They celebrate your evolution rather than fearing it. They celebrate your evolution and support your growth.

RESPECT IN ACTION

They honor your time, body, boundaries, and voice. Respect shows up in daily behaviors, not empty promises.

SAFETY AND CALM

Their presence regulates your nervous system. Real love feels grounding, not like walking on eggshells.

ACCOUNTABILITY

They own mistakes without blaming, deflecting, or rewriting the story. Growth requires truth.

INTEGRITY

They live aligned with their values, follow through on promises, and act with honesty even when no one is watching.

End of Week 2 Reflection

BUILD

THEME | REBUILDING YOUR INNER FOUNDATION

1. What belief or behavior no longer aligns with the version of me I'm becoming?

- *The belief that I need to prove my worth to be chosen.*
- *The pattern of minimizing my needs to maintain peace.*

2. What pattern did I finally recognize and begin to disrupt?

- *People-pleasing at the cost of my peace.*
- *Emotionally chasing those who pull away.*

3. What emotional needs have kept me in relationships at the cost of my well-being?

- *The need to be seen and how I validate myself instead of seeking external approval.*
- *The need for financial security that kept me in disrespect.*

Mini Grounding Reminder:

You're not just healing from what happened, you're building something new. Every pattern you've questioned, every boundary you've set, every moment you chose yourself, you're becoming who you were always meant to be.

You've now practiced *The 21·7·7·7 Method* for 14 days, and it's becoming part of you.

This structure isn't just a healing Method, it's a way back to your truth, every time.

Acceptance

It's recognizing the injustice, the betrayal, the harm and still choosing to move toward the future. It's choosing what's best for you. It's understanding that some people are simply not capable of seeing the truth, shaped by their own unresolved wounds. It's letting the pain be only a piece of your story without *Allowing* it to shape your future. You no longer need an apology to move on, because you understand they were never capable of truly understanding.

You made the decision to stop pouring energy into conversations that were never meant to lead to resolution. You stopped explaining yourself to those unwilling to meet you with understanding. You chose peace over proving your point.

Acceptance is emotional maturity, the kind that lets you create your own closure, without waiting to feel fully understood, ready or healed before moving forward.

It's trusting that the universe sees farther than you can and that what's meant for you is already making its way to you. It's believing that those who caused harm will face what they're meant to, in their own time, and without your involvement. It's the quiet courage to look at what broke you and say: *"Yes, that was real. Yes, it was hard. But it revealed the wounds I still carried and reminded me of my worth."*

Healing doesn't always arrive in forgiveness. Sometimes, it's the quiet decision to stop waiting for accountability that may never come. It's no longer needing them to understand—because you finally understand yourself. And you wish them well, because you trust the process.

You choose your peace. Your *healing.* Your next chapter.

And with all of it, you begin again.
Wiser. Softer. Still *standing.*

PHASE 3
RISE

DAYS 15–21 | THE RETURN TO SELF

You've faced the truth. You've rewired the patterns. Now—you *Rise.*
In this phase, healing becomes embodiment. You're no longer reacting from pain, you're choosing from clarity. You're not looking back. You're moving forward—stepping into who you're becoming with more clarity, more calm, and more confidence.

This is where your healing becomes direction:

- You rebuild self-trust from within.
- You honor your desires without shame.
- You reinforce boundaries without guilt.
- You recognize safe *love* when it appears.
- You lead from truth, not trauma.
- You create from wholeness, not wounds.
- You let desire, *shape what comes next.*

It's not about moving on from pain. It's about walking forward with clear eyes. Carrying the lesson, and no longer willing to betray yourself for hope given away to someone who never earned it.

You're not who you were when this began. And now, you move differently—rooted, evolved, and unwilling to negotiate your value ever again.

If at any given time this feels overwhelming, give yourself permission to stop and take a grounding breath.

TRACE SYSTEM

Weekly Intention Prompt:

This week, I no longer operate from ______________________________, I rise into peace.

This is the work of transformation: the slow, steady choice to rise beyond old patterns into a new way of being. From chasing to leading. From survival to alignment. From proving to living in truth. From fear to clarity. Each shift supports your movement from the old self into the woman who protects her peace, honors her worth, and walks in clarity.

Intention

You've reclaimed your voice, your clarity, your needs. Now you practice living from that place daily. This is about fully becoming her—the higher version of you who protects her peace, honors her needs, and walks in strength. You don't chase anymore. You lead with standards.

Micro-Habits to Choose From

Choose 1 to 3. Track 1 or 2 daily.

- Redirected energy toward my goals
- Protected my valuable time
- I acted like the woman I'm becoming
- Made a decision without defending it
- I didn't shrink to be understood
- I didn't justify my wants or needs

HABITS	SUN	MON	TUE	WED	THU	FRI	SAT

One gentle action each day. One aligned decision at a time.

Day 15 — The Return to Inner Authority

Release *.7 min*

How often did you silence what you truly felt just to keep the peace? Reflect on the times you walked on eggshells, not because you lacked strength, but because you feared the cost of speaking your truth. How many times did you say, "You're right," just to avoid conflict, even when you knew they weren't? Explore the moments you were made to feel small, called "too sensitive," "ungrateful," or "negative" for simply speaking your truth. Name the pattern of self-abandonment: the quiet ways you kept betraying your voice to preserve connection. Then begin rewriting it.

Reframe *.7 min*

You gave your power away to keep the peace, but your truth was never too much. You were conditioned to doubt your voice because it disrupted the comfort of someone who needed control, and made to believe that speaking up would cost you love. *Break this belief:* You don't need permission to speak. Your voice is valid, even when it's inconvenient or doesn't align with theirs. *New lens:* real love does not punish truth; it makes space for it, respects it, and welcomes it.

Rewire *.7 min*

I trust my inner values and principles to guide me. I honor my voice as valid and worthy of being heard. I stand rooted in my power, fully, clearly, and with unwavering strength.

D

D

Day 16 — Trusting Your Growth

Release *.7 min*

How did this relationship shape the woman you are now? What do you see clearly now that you couldn't see then about your worth, your voice, your limits? How has pain sharpened your self-respect? In what ways do you now honor your truth more fully, speak it more clearly, protect it more fiercely? What boundaries exist now that were once unthinkable? What does the older version of you finally feel safe enough to become? List every way this experience became a turning point in how you love, how you live, and how you stand for yourself. Let the lessons reveal themselves: pain can be a teacher, clarity a gift, and wisdom the proof that you have risen stronger.

Reframe *.7 min*

You are not the same person who entered that relationship. The pain you survived became wisdom you now carry. Every red flag you missed taught you what to watch for. Every boundary you didn't have then, you have now. *Break this belief:* that because you got hurt, and that this relationship only ruined your life. *New lens:* that relationship did not end your story. It revealed what needed healing and gifted you profound wisdom for what comes next. You are fundamentally different now.

Rewire *.7 min*

I trust my growth. I am not the same person who would accept what I used to accept. The wisdom I gained from this pain is real, and it protects me moving forward.

D

D

Landing Softly

A RITUAL FOR THE RESTLESS NIGHTS

Not all healing happens in the light of day. Sometimes, clarity lands but the nervous system still loops. Sometimes, you've written the truth but your body hasn't caught up. Sometimes, peace feels near but sleep feels far. These moments are not signs of regression but signals that your system is still processing.

Healing is not linear, and neither is regulation.

This isn't a step backward. It's your nervous system doing exactly what it was designed to do: protect you. When the mind senses unresolved pain or ambiguity, it loops to seek completion or resolution. Rumination is often the brain's way of trying to resolve unfinished emotional business, especially in the absence of closure. Your body holds the memory even when your mind understands the lesson, and that's not a setback. It's intelligence.

Night Safety is a space to soften the spiral. It meets you in that in–between when you've done the work but still feel the weight. It's where logic fades and emotion lingers. A one–page ritual to interrupt the noise, ground your system, and gently redirect your mind toward rest. Use it anytime the quiet feels too loud. When you need direction but the answers can wait. Let it be your soft place to land. A reset, not a rescue. A practice of remembering: you are already safe enough to rest.

Night Safety

1. Write | *2. Resolve* | *3. Direct*

As the work deepens, so must your rest. The following tool is your evening ritual for emotional release and nervous system reset. Night Safety is a trauma-informed, neuroscience-aligned evening ritual for the nights your mind refuses to let go. In one page, it offloads emotional weight, interrupts spirals, and restores the body to calm. Rooted in the sequence *Write · Resolve · Direct,* it gives the mind what it craves most in overwhelm: a way forward. When you're carrying heartbreak, decision fatigue, invisible grief, or simply the weight of a life in motion, the mind loops in search of safety. Research shows rumination is the brain's attempt to hold on until it senses resolution. What it needs is *direction*—even when nothing is fully resolved.

Born at 3:30 a.m. in a season when the spirals wouldn't stop, this tool isn't deep processing—it's emotional first aid. A simple three-step sequence that names what's heavy, restores orientation, and anchors the body in felt safety. Studies show pre-sleep journaling can significantly reduce mental looping, especially when it ends with resolution or clearly defined next steps. Night Safety isn't about reflection or insight. It's about closure—a way to end the day so the nervous system can finally exhale. Because when the mind spirals at night, it isn't trying to overthink. It's trying to feel safe.

THE SEQUENCE

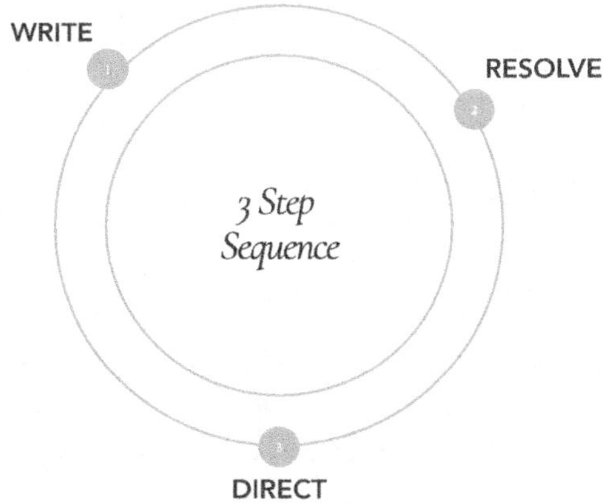

1

Getting thoughts out of your head and onto paper reduces mental load. The mind is wired for resolution, it loops until it sees what it's trying to solve. Name what feels unresolved: the problems, the unfinished, the uncertain.

2

Once the loop is on paper, the brain automatically seeks resolution. Show the mind a way forward, a plan, a small direction, a clear action. Even the simplest solution reminds the mind that a way forward exists.

3

After finding resolution, close the night by choosing how to carry forward. Anchor your system in certainty and direction. Close the loop with reassurance: this is enough for tonight. There is a path. There is a path unfolding. You are safe to rest.

Night Safety: Sequence

1. Write | *2. Resolve* | *3. Direct*

This is the Night Safety sequence. Clear, grounded, and rooted in both lived experience and neuroscience-informed care. You're not here to solve everything tonight. You're offering your mind just enough resolution to quiet the spiral. By allowing it to land on the page, you're signaling to your nervous system that it's safe to soften. Not because the pain has disappeared, but because you no longer need to carry it alone. Safe enough to pause. Safe enough to rest.

1 WRITE

Let the loop name unfold. Without judgment.

"I lost my job today. I'm replaying the conversation over and over, their words, my words, the way it ended. My chest feels tight and my mind keeps asking how I'll cover my rent.
I keep looping through every worst-case scenario, trying to figure out how to fix it."

Write what feels unresolved. Let the page hold it.

2 RESOLVE

Offer the mind direction—a plan—even a small one.

"Tomorrow I'll ask my family for support and update my resume before noon. I'll list three people to contact for leads and send the first message mid-afternoon. These steps will help me feel steady and remind me I'm moving forward, even if everything isn't solved tonight."

Offer one clear action, solution to move forward.

3 DIRECT

Signal the body that it's safe to let go.

"Losing my job is not losing my worth. Everything happens for a reason, and I always land on my feet. I didn't even like that job, this might be the beginning of something better. I can already feel my body exhale. This day is complete. My body can now rest. I am safe in this moment."

You are safe tonight. The path is unfolding.

If you need more space, use this page. Let it hold the spirals, the unresolved edges, the weight your mind can't put down. Name what's circling, offer it direction, and let the page carry what you no longer need to hold alone.

1. Write | ***2. Resolve*** | ***3. Direct***

1 WRITE

Let the loop name unfold. Without judgment.

2 RESOLVE

Offer the mind direction—a plan—even a small one.

3 DIRECT

Signal the body that it's safe to let go.

D

Day 17 — Safe Love Starts With Me

Release *.7 min*

What does safe, healthy, emotionally grounded love feel like in a relationship and what will you no longer settle for? What kind of presence, energy, and behavior makes you feel deeply seen, cherished, and emotionally safe? How has your understanding of love evolved and what do you now require for it to feel true, steady, and aligned? Write your vision for recognizing and welcoming safe connection and the healed version of you who is strong, clear, and ready to receive it.

Reframe *.7 min*

When you feel safe, you can love freely. You don't have to fear connection, you just need to discern between confusion and emotional safety. Safe love is steady, spacious, and deeply fulfilling. You can desire deep connection without ever compromising your peace, your standards, or your voice. Break this belief: that intensity equals depth, or that calm love lacks passion. New lens: Real passion rises from emotional safety. It's the stillness that allows your nervous system to soften, and your heart to feel at home.

Rewire *.7 min*

I open my heart where peace, respect, and consistency are present. I welcome love that feels safe, honors my voice, and meets me with clarity and care.

Revisit your Relationship Standard from Day 14 and notice how this vision aligns.

D

D

D

Day 18 — The Power of Saying No

Release *.7 min*

Where in your life are you still saying yes to keep the peace instead of saying no to protect yourself? What relationships drain you, yet you maintain them out of guilt? What commitments do you continue simply to avoid disappointing others? Where do you override your own discomfort to preserve harmony at the expense of your well-being? What situations exhaust your energy, yet you stay and endure them anyway? What would you walk away from immediately if you no longer feared being seen as difficult or unkind?

Reframe *.7 min*

You were conditioned to believe kindness meant being endlessly available, that your needs mattered less than other people's comfort. But being a good person was never meant to cost you your peace. *Break this belief:* that setting boundaries makes you difficult or unkind. *New lens:* Those who care for you will honor your limits, not guilt you for having them. And each time you choose what protects your peace, you teach the world how to meet you with the respect you've always deserved.

Rewire *.7 min*

My boundaries are sacred and require no explanation. I protect my energy without justification, because my peace is essential. The right people meet my limits with care, not question.

D

D

D

Day 19 — Your Wants Are Not Too Much

Release *.7 min*

What is truly important to me in life, in love, and in who I am becoming? What do I value so deeply that I refuse to compromise it again? What kind of partnership aligns with my truth, not my fear of being alone? What traits, energies, or dynamics pull me out of myself, and what do I now walk away from the moment it no longer aligns? This is self-loyalty. Name your values. Write them clearly, so your mind, body, and heart recognize them as non-negotiable. Trust yourself enough to leave when they are not honored.

Reframe *.7 min*

Your deepest values reveal what truly matters to you. What you hold as principle in life, love, and partnership reflects what your soul is wired to honor. *Break this belief:* that you must compromise your values to be loved or lower your standards to be chosen. *New lens:* values are core truth. The clearer you are about them, the easier it becomes to walk away from anything that does not align.

Rewire *.7 min*

I trust what I value because it reflects my truth. I no longer edit my needs to fit what is available. I choose only what aligns. What matters to me is not negotiable. It guides me toward the life and love I am meant to receive.

Carry these values forward into your Relationship Standard in Day 14. Love that is true will never require you to betray what you hold as truth.

D

D

D

Day 20 — Rising From Knowing

Release .7 *min*

What are the foundations you now know you must build for yourself—whether financial security, emotional safety, stability, or other protections you once sought in others? Name where you are no longer waiting for someone else to provide what you can now create within. Release the belief that your peace, protection, or stability depends on another's presence or participation, and allow yourself to see the pillars you are ready to build from your own strength.

Reframe .7 *min*

This experience has revealed what I must now create and protect within myself. I see clearly the foundations I need to build—whether financial security, emotional safety, stability, or the kind of protection I once searched for in others. These are no longer things I wait to be given to me, they are now my mission to cultivate. *Break this belief:* that I need someone else to provide the safety, security, or stability that anchors my life. *New lens:* I rise knowing what I bring to the table and what I will no longer outsource. I build the pillars of my own future, rooted in self-sufficiency, vision, and truth. My growth is no longer dependent on what others can give me—it is carried by the strength I am creating within myself.

Rewire .7 *min*

My safety, stability, and growth are no longer outsourced. My future is carried by my own strength, vision, and truth, anchored in the foundations I am building every day.

D

Day 21 — This is Noclosure

Release *.7 min*

Noclosure is the quiet work of noticing the shifts already taking root within you. The evidence that healing is unfolding, even when silence remains. Reflect on what you have begun to learn, process, and release along this journey. Consider the conversations you are no longer waiting for, the explanations you have stopped needing because you now understand their limitations, and the misunderstandings you are no longer compelled to correct. Explore the beliefs you have started to outgrow, the patterns you have broken, and the new vision you now hold about love, worth, and relationships. Notice the ways you are beginning to show up differently and imagine the future you are building, one that has nothing to do with their understanding. Write about how you are becoming your own closure and why their participation is no longer required for your peace.

Reframe *.7 min*

You don't need to be understood by people who chose not to understand you, or who refused to take responsibility. You don't need to explain yourself to those who hurt you and decided you were the problem. You don't need their validation, their apology, or their acknowledgment to move forward. *Break this belief:* that you need their recognition to trust your own truth, or their participation to find peace. *New lens:* Your healing is unfolding without them. Your growth is happening despite them. Your Noclosure is not dependent on them. It is born from your own hard-earned strength, integrity, and truth.

Rewire *.7 min*

This is Noclosure. I am no longer waiting for conversations that will never happen or apologies that will never come. I choose to build my future on the foundation of who I am becoming, not on the ruins of what broke me.

D

D

D

End of Week 3 Reflection

RISE

THEME | THE RETURN TO SELF

1. What boundary did I honor, and how did it shift my energy or deepen my sense of peace?

- *I didn't respond right away, and felt peace instead of panic.*
- *I ended a draining conversation, and noticed my breath soften.*

2. What decision or choice came from clarity instead of fear this week?

- *I chose rest without guilt.*
- *I unfollowed someone who made me question my worth.*

3. What part of me do I promise to keep protecting and honoring?

- *The voice that whispers the truth, even when it's inconvenient.*
- *My peace, because I finally understand how rare and sacred it is.*

Mini Grounding Reminder:

You didn't just survive this transformation, you led it. This daily 21–minute rhythm wasn't just healing, it was a reclamation. Through *the 21·7·7·7 Method*, you have trained your system to choose peace, truth, and power again and again. You are living proof that people can change, grow, and choose themselves.

You are your safest home. Keep choosing you.

Noclosure

THE JOURNAL THAT HEALS WHAT WAS LEFT UNFINISHED

Noclosure was born for the endings that offered no answers, the silences that were never filled, and the goodbyes that left more ache than peace. It exists for the moments when conversations remain unfinished, accountability is denied, and apologies are never offered. This is not about waiting. This is not about persuading. This is about reclaiming.

This isn't just the end of a journal. It is the end of forgetting your own worth, the end of apologizing, of staying quiet to keep the peace, of dimming yourself to make others comfortable. For 21 days, you have faced what most people run from their entire lives. You have processed pain, released the weight of old wounds, and sat with truth even when it hurt. You let the silence speak. You held your own *heart* when no one else did. You released the version of yourself that begged to be chosen. You rewired the belief that love must be earned. And you rose from the ashes of a relationship that was never built to meet you, stepping into a version of yourself that is whole, unwavering, and undeniably you.

Let this page be your line in the sand. You are no longer available for what depletes you. You are not someone to be almost loved. You are here, fully present, grounded, and empowered. These words are no longer just prompts—they are your truth.

The Noclosure Method is what has guided you through what others left unresolved. It offered you a structure to *Release* what was never yours to carry, to *Reframe* what once defined you, and to *Rewire* your story from the inside out. Through the 21·7·7·7 rhythm, you have retrained your system to choose allowing over proving, clarity over their narrative, and healing over stagnation—again and again. You have built the quiet strength to stop waiting for apologies or explanations that will never come, to trust your own process, and to create your peace from within. Your healing is unfolding without them. Your growth is rising despite them. Your peace is created beyond them.

This journal does not end here. *The 21·7·7·7 Method*, along with each of the tools you've practiced, is not only for these 21 days—it is your foundation for life. A rhythm of living you can return to whenever clarity feels far away, whenever silence feels heavy, whenever you need to remember who you are. *Noclosure* is beyond every pain you have endured. It is the turning point where inner healing meets self-recognition, where you reclaim your worth, define your standards, and choose how you allow yourself to be treated. It is not the end of something—it is the beginning of becoming.

With fierce love. With quiet power. With a *soul* that remembers.

IDENTITY WORK
BECOMING

MANIFESTATION THROUGH IDENTITY

You've made it through. Not just through the journal, but through the hardest part: the truth-telling, the unraveling and the letting go.

Now begins the most important part of healing: who you become from here. This phase is about building—the daily decisions, the new identity, the version of you who no longer reacts from pain but leads from clarity.

Healing doesn't end when the pain softens. That's when it begins to take root. Because healing isn't just emotional—it's structural. It's physical. It's environmental. It's behavioral. It shows up in your habits. In your home. In the boundaries you hold, the relationships you choose, and the way you live your life.

This is where you create a foundation for your future self. Not just in theory, in *action*. You'll now be guided through the Compound Becoming System, a framework to help you embody this new version of you. The one who:

- Lives with *intention.*
- Has standards that match her self-worth.
- Doesn't abandon herself to be understood.
- Builds a life that protects her peace, instead of recovering from its absence.

Small shifts. Real actions. Clear standards. Because change doesn't happen in your head, it happens in your habits.

And know this: sometimes, the most painful endings are the ones that redirect us. That relationship may have broken you, but it also revealed you. It taught you something. About your worth. About your values. About your boundaries. Your trust. Your standards.

This wasn't just a heartbreak.
It was a wake-up call, for the life you're now ready to build. You're not who you were.
You're becoming who you were always meant to be.

The 21 Lines

If you haven't already completed it, you are invited to turn to page 169. 21 Lines I Will Live By is your identity code. A set of self defined principles that reflect the woman you have become. Each line captures a life standard you now choose to live by.

Not just reflections, but non-negotiables. The things you no longer tolerate. The truth you stand in. The values you protect. By the end, you'll have a clear map of who you now are. Grounded, intentional, and unmistakably you.

Welcome to the Compound Becoming phase.

A Season of Becoming

BECOMING THE STANDARD

This isn't a vision exercise. It's a declaration. You're not manifesting from hope. You're anchoring into identity—the version of you who no longer waits to be picked, validated, or pursued.

You don't perform worth. You embody it. You've done the work. You've faced yourself. You've healed in silence. Now, you move differently. You no longer entertain confusion, inconsistency, or those who settle for comfort over growth. Not because you're guarded, but because you're clear.

It's about having high standards. Rooted in self-respect and maturity not ego. You've worked too hard to heal and become your best self to hand that version of you to just anyone passing by.

You have boundaries. You have clarity. You don't have time for emotional shortcuts, time-wasters, or half-effort connections. You know exactly what you want, and you don't apologize for it. You don't chase alignment, you create it, through who you are, what you allow, and what you walk away from without explanation.

Anyone who enters your life now meets you in truth—or not at all. You're no longer proving anything. You're not here to be chosen—you're here to choose. You don't explain your worth. You live by it. And anything that doesn't align, exits quietly.

This is the season where the work becomes rhythm.
Where healing moves from the page into your days, where aligned actions replace old reactions.
Where clarity becomes your compass, and devotion becomes your momentum.

A decision, every morning: to no longer live from the version of you who forgot her worth. To see yourself clearly. To honor what you value. To choose, again and again, to live from the version of you who is building something real.

It won't happen all at once. Growth is a season. A layering, a sculpting, a slow becoming.
This is the season of construction: steady, intentional, alive.

There will be seasons of stillness, of unraveling, of not knowing. And then, seasons of returning, of remembering, of rising.
Because you don't just wake up and become the butterfly. You rise into her, little by little.

My Standards Moving Forward

FROM SURVIVAL TO STANDARDS

You don't just heal from the relationship. You heal the version of yourself that accepted what came with it. *Noclosure* healing is an act of radical self-respect. It reveals what most healing paths miss: when closure isn't offered, you face deeper truths, the wounds, beliefs, and survival patterns that kept you attached.

When there's no apology, no explanation, and no resolution, you're left with silence. But within that silence is something powerful: the opportunity to choose what's truly best for you. To stop chasing clarity from unhealthy dynamics. To build *resilience.* And to understand that healing doesn't require another conversation. It requires a decision. A decision to choose peace over pain. Self-worth over confusion. And yourself, above all.

We've been taught to mistake intensity for connection—to chase sparks instead of safety. But real love, the kind you choose after healing, is something deeper. It's the willingness to face your own triggers, to unlearn toxic patterns, and to show up with emotional maturity.

It's not built on ease or excitement, but on conscious commitment, a choice to grow, to evolve, and to keep showing up, even when it's inconvenient. And because that work was hard-won, you no longer grant easy access to your energy. You filter with discernment and deep self-respect, because now you know: peace is something you protect.

As I move forward—I carry self-respect, high standards, and peace. I choose relationships that are consistent, safe, and grounded. I stop chasing emotional highs and start honoring emotional health. This is what I value now:

- Accountability over charm
- Clarity over chemistry
- Safety over sparks
- Repair over avoidance
- How I'm treated over how much I care

This is the version of me that has learned the wisdom. She's no longer waiting to be chosen. She chooses herself—and accepts nothing less than what aligns with that.

Compound Becoming System

MANIFESTATION = VISION -> IDENTITY -> ALIGNED ACTION

This is Compound Becoming, because small, consistent identity shifts compound over time to create inevitable transformation.

It's not about visualizing outcomes or pasting images onto vision boards. It's about setting specific, measurable objectives—paired with daily execution rituals that build momentum in your favor.

It's about becoming through your habits—how you feel, focus, act, and decide daily, in service of a clear and defined result: your becoming.

Becoming isn't a wish. It's a system. A clear set of goals, habits, and strategic shifts, powered by consistent action and unwavering clarity of vision.

Now, it's time to live the healing, not just feel it.

This is where you stop circling the wound and start building from the wisdom it gave you. This is where structure meets embodiment. Where your peace becomes a system. Where you no longer just survive. You create.

Alignment

Compound Becoming is the structure that turns healing into how you live, not just how you feel.

This framework is built on one quiet truth: small, repeated shifts in habits and actions don't just shape behavior—they initiate transformation. Not through hope, but through clarity, self-honoring standards, and consistent action.

When clear intention meets aligned behavior, you stop waiting for life to shift and start living in alignment with your growth. One goal per area, actions anchored in who you're rising into supported by the systems that sustain becoming.

The Process

- Vision → What do I truly want?
- Identity → Who am I when this is already real?
- Aligned Action → What daily choices build this reality?

On the following page, the Becoming begins. Choose the areas that hold the most weight in this season of your Becoming. Define each desire with clarity and intention, then meet them with aligned, consistent, and repeated action.

This is how transformation manifests: when aligned choices align with hope. When who you're becoming is no longer a vision, but a rhythm, led by action, shaped by devotion, lived as truth.

One clear decision. One grounded devotion. One Becoming at a time.

Living from your Healing

You are not chasing your future self. You are practicing her. You are entering the energy of the woman who already lives the life you are building. Becoming her means honoring her thoughts, her boundaries, and her standards. It means prioritizing your healing and regulating your nervous system, allowing calm to feel safe rather than unfamiliar. It means releasing survival mode and choosing from who you are becoming. Before you answer, pause and breathe slowly. Let your system settle into the version of you who lives in alignment, acts with intention, and shapes her days in service of her higher self.

Reflection Prompts for Becoming

1. What does the future me believe about herself that I'm learning to believe now?

2. What boundary or standard protects her peace, and am I ready to live by it?

3. What habit no longer aligns with who I'm becoming, and am I ready to release it?

4. What decision or project have I been avoiding, and what would self-trust choose now?

5. What habit do I need to stop repeating, because it no longer aligns with who I'm becoming?

Money & Work

Vision

Sustainable income shaped by integrity and confidence.

Ex: $10K/month from 3 clients, 25h/week.

Identity

Rooted. Strategic. Boundaried. She leads with clarity and delivers with excellence.

Own my value. Set rates without explanation.

Aligned Action

1. Monday morning CEO hour: planning, priorities
2. Two quality outreach connections per week

Health & Body

Vision

A body that feels energized, healthy, and respected.

Ex: Move 4x/week. Lose 10 lbs over 3 months.

Identity

Disciplined with grace. Prioritizes rest and movement equally.

I choose discipline. I move and rest intentionally.

Aligned Action

1. 30 minutes of intentional movement, 4x/week
2. Meal prep ritual every Sunday

Love & Relationships

Vision

A secure, emotionally mature partnership rooted in respect and reciprocity.

A relationship that feels consistent and safe.

Identity

Respects herself deeply. No longer compromises clarity for chemistry.

Walk away from confusion. Value presence.

Aligned Action

1. How does this connection make me feel?
2. No time for emotionally unavailable people.

Personal Growth & HealingVision

Vision

A regulated nervous system and a deep connection to your inner peace.

Calm in conflict. Less reactive. Rewiring patterns.

Identity

Grounded. Self-aware. She feels, reflects, then moves.

Notices triggers. Pauses before reacting.

Aligned Action

1. Weekly reflection on one recurring emotional loop.
2. 1x/week intentional learning: podcast, reading.

21 Lines I Will Live By

Your New Principles. One shift. One truth. One new standard per day.

1

2

3

4

5

6

7

8

9

10

11

12

13

14

15

16

17

18

19

20

21

21 standards going forward. No negotiation.

Sometimes life doesn't fall apart. It clears the path that was always meant for you.
You loved with your whole heart.
You gave more than you had.
And somewhere along the way, you began to disappear inside someone else's story.
It didn't fall apart. It exposed what was never whole.
A quiet redirection.
The kind that hurts first, then frees you.
Because real wisdom doesn't always arrive gently.
It's carved from rupture.
And in that ending, something unshakable surfaced:
your self–trust. Your quiet strength.
your refusal to abandon yourself again. Your knowing.
This wasn't just heartbreak. It was a turning point.
A truth you couldn't have reached any other way.
The slow forging of your resilience.
The clarity that being chosen means nothing if you keep losing yourself to stay.
This is for the you who no longer makes herself smaller to fit inside someone else's comfort.
Who doesn't confuse staying with safety.
Who no longer sees endings as evidence of unworthiness, but as part of the shaping. Because now you know:
not everyone is meant to stay,
but every chapter was part of becoming the woman you were always meant to be.

Closing Note

You didn't just finish a journal. You completed a promise. A quiet promise to return to yourself, and you did. You showed up for your healing when it would have been easier to numb it. You stayed when it was uncomfortable. You faced truths you once tried to bury. And step by step, you *reclaimed* yourself.

You have proven to yourself that you are not defined by what happened to you. By closing this chapter with intention, you are sending a message to the universe:

I am no longer available for anything that does not honor my worth. I am clearing space for what is meant for me to find me.

Healing isn't just about feeling better. It's about honoring the perspective you've gained and recognizing what the experience taught you. It's the clarity that comes from reflection, from looking inward with *honesty.*

It's how you begin to break generational cycles, rebuild your foundation, and see yourself and others through wiser, more compassionate eyes. It's what helps you spot red flags sooner, choose love that nourishes you, build friendships rooted in truth, and finally live a life aligned with your deepest self. We don't attract what we want. We attract what needs healing. And then, what we're finally ready for.

By completing this journal, by choosing healing, you're not just closing a chapter, you're opening yourself to everything beautiful that's still ahead. You didn't leave because you stopped loving them. You left because you finally started loving yourself, and realized you were meant for more.

From here on, you are no longer waiting for closure, permission, or validation. You carry your own peace. You trust your own voice. You build your own future. You're no longer who you were. You're who you decide to become. And this is just the *beginning.*

Self–Love Contract

THE CLOSURE I WAS NEVER GIVEN. FROM HER

I worked too hard for my peace. No one gets in unless they're aligned, intentional, and real. If it's not mutual, consistent, and clear, it's out. No matter how good it looks.

My Promise to Myself:

I promise to remain loyal to myself. I release the need for closure from what could not meet me with clarity and responsibility. I close this chapter with conviction. From here, I move forward in alignment, building myself across every dimension of becoming, aesthetic, spiritual, emotional, and intellectual. Through the habits I choose and the standards I live by, my emotional healing becomes a daily practice, lived with intention. This is no longer about what ended. It is about what begins.

Date: ....

Signature: ....

Don't Look Back

The past has nothing new to tell you.
If it cost you your peace, it was never love.
Even if they come back.
Even if they say all the right things.

Your nervous system remembers
what your heart once tried to forget.

You don't need to reopen
what you fought so hard to close.

You don't need to lose yourself again
just to see if they've changed.

Some people aren't your future.
They were your turning point. A lesson.
And every time you revisit the past,
you delay what's already trying to find you.
Let it go.

Allow it to remain a chapter you've outgrown,
one you no longer need to edit or explain.
You are not who you were.
And now, you get to choose from truth and alignment.

What's meant for you will meet you in your wholeness,
not your wounds.

You're not starting over.
You're starting wiser.
As someone who finally knows her worth...
and *protects it.*

Continue the *Journey*

This is where your healing expands

You've completed the 21-Day *Noclosure Method,* a profound act of courage, commitment, and self-respect. This is not the end. Healing continues through tools that deepen the practice, rituals that sustain the rise, and a community that honors your pace and holds space with *care.*

What Awaits You Next

Scan the QR code to join instantly:

TOOL	DESCRIPTION
COMPANION TOOLKIT	An intentional collection—Spiral Reset, 21 Lines I Will Live By, and Trace Tracker, created to carry the work beyond these pages.
THE RISING JOURNEY COMMUNITY	A safe space to connect, share, and rise with women walking the same path. Be first to access the Rising Journey App when it launches.

The Rising Journey Community

A safe space to share what hurts, feel seen, and heal alongside women who truly understand.

- Share what hurts, without judgment.
- Evolve and Heal, in the middle, not just the breakthrough.
- Feel seen, because someone else gets it.

If you've ever wished you had someone to vent to, cry with, or simply say 'me too,' this is the space we're creating.

→ Search "Rising Journey Community" on Facebook
→ Or scan the QR below to request access

This is not about performing healing. It's about feeling safe while you live it.

About the Creator

FOUNDER OF RISING JOURNEY. CREATOR OF A SCIENCE-ALIGNED HEALING FRAMEWORK FOR NOCLOSURE.

Rising Journey was created to establish a new standard for healing after unresolved endings. Healing built on structure, consistency, and direction. Hassania is the founder of Rising Journey and the creator of a science-aligned framework for emotional healing. Her work addresses a critical gap in how heartbreak is treated: pain is acknowledged, but rarely given a process. Time is expected to heal, yet time alone offers no structure, safety, or direction.

Drawing on years of research in trauma-informed care, nervous system regulation, and behavior-based change, Hassania developed a daily, structured method that treats healing as an intentional practice rather than a passive waiting period.

Rising Journey serves those navigating heartbreak, separation, and unresolved endings who are ready for more than reassurance. Through guided structure, daily practice, and clear internal standards, the work supports a shift from emotional survival to emotional leadership. Healing here is not measured by time, but by the structure you maintain and the standards you build.

One reset. One return. One Rise at a time.

Coming Soon: The Rising Journey App

> Imagine a space that holds you through the spiral.
> A real-time tool that helps you pause, ground, reflect, and return to your truth.
>
> We're building it. And when it's ready, you'll be the first to know.

Rising Journey Inc.

From journal to journey. From ink to embodiment.
From sacred reflection to real-time support.
These closing pages carry the imprint of Rising Journey's next evolution, a digital sanctuary designed to rise with you, wherever you are.

Rising Journey

Rising Journey Community

@risingjourney.co

hello@risingjourney.co

Made in the USA
Monee, IL
13 September 2026

63176222R00103